		DATE DUE	

Rising to the Occasion

RISING *to the* OCCASION

A Practical Companion for the Occasionally Perplexed

EDITH HAZARD & WALLACE PINFOLD

❖

Algonquin Books of Chapel Hill

1993

OUACHITA TECHNICAL COLLEGE

Published by
ALGONQUIN BOOKS OF CHAPEL HILL
Post Office Box 2225
Chapel Hill, North Carolina 27515-2225

a division of
Workman Publishing
708 Broadway
New York, New York 10003

LIBRARY OF CONGRESS
CATALOGING-IN-PUBLICATION DATA

Hazard, Edith.
Rising to the occasion: a practical companion for the occasionally
perplexed / Edith Hazard and Wallace Pinfold.
p.   cm.
ISBN 1-56512-029-9
1. Home economics. 2. Etiquette. I. Pinfold, Wallace. II. Title.
TX147,H36   1993
640—dc20   92-44994
CIP

6   8   10   9   7

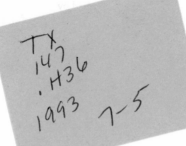
This book is dedicated to our mothers.

Contents

We gratefully acknowledge the encouragement, support, and professional advice generously given to us by Angus III, Duncan, and James King, Jim Pinfold and Frances Phillips, Fleet Van Riper, Sonia Hodgkins, Angus King, Jr., Hilary Innis, David Kew, Jim Dodson, Jennifer Walsh, Elisabeth Scharlatt, Julia Boss, Virginia Holman, Eric, Mary, and Elizabeth Butler, Ray Fortin of Autometrics, Inc., Martha Hermance, Robert Shepherd, Fraser Ruwet, C. Bruce Hazard, Deborah Hart, Hervey Tessier, and David Violet.

To the Gentle Reader:

What are the consequences of preparing an undercooked egg? proposing an awkward toast? presenting a poorly wrapped gift? Not much, really, when you stack them up against the consequences of misusing a very sharp knife, misreading the circuit breaker, or misplacing the jumper cables. We begin, then with a note of caution: when you come to instructions involving the use of sharp tools and electric currents, blazing fires and deep water, do be sure to follow each step with considerable thought and utmost care.

—E.H. and W.P.

Rising to the Occasion

PREFACE

❖

When your grandfather was a boy, he walked several miles to school, often through snowdrifts that came up to his chest. He carried many books and did more homework than you and your parents combined ever did. Your grandmother made all her own clothes and she, too, walked through drifting snow to do it. Your grandparents may have grown up in southern California or Poland, southern Italy or on a farm in western Massachusetts, but it seems to make no difference: they all had the same childhood. Some things never change.

Others do. Skills that once were common now are scarce. Abilities that were so much a part of every adult's repertoire that they went unnoticed now are greeted with amazement or gratitude or both. A woman we know entered college in 1936, having never before met a Democrat. When her son graduated from college in 1968, he didn't know a single vegetarian. Now, on the cusp of the year 2000, vegetarians are almost as common as Democrats.

Theoretically, you've grown up in a different world from the one in which your parents did. Minor social graces—dancing the waltz, writing a thank-you note, and so forth—thought to be the product of "the advantages" one may have had didn't get passed on to you because your parents were so busy making a living or finding themselves they didn't have time. Practical skills once so ordinary they weren't given a second thought—laying a fire, unclogging a sink—have also fallen by the wayside. Skills, knacks, and talents once found in all kinds of people's repertoires are now scarce as hen's teeth.

What happened? Changes in the workplace happened. Reconfiguration of sex roles happened. History happened. Why should this be so? Because if some things never change, the times do. It used to be that Mom roasted the turkey and Dad carved. Dad took out the garbage and Mom ironed his shirts. Certain domestic tasks were men's work, others belonged exclusively to women. Boy children and girl children were taught to observe and do likewise. But for reasons complicated enough to constitute the subject of entire books, the way we use time changed. Mom went to work outside the home. Dad stayed at work. No one had the time or energy to teach the next generation the things they had learned from their own parents. Later, when it became politically incorrect to differentiate between women's work and men's, everyone ended up doing everything. After a fashion.

It's nobody's fault. Often, two-income families became one-income families when Mom and Dad divorced. This put time at an even greater premium. One person now had to do all the remunerative work, all the chores, all the shopping, and all the cooking formerly done by two. During the 1980s, when the American economy was booming, some people found a partial solution to their dilemma in services. Take-out food, company cars, laundries that delivered, housecleaners, even people to walk the dog were greeted with open arms and checkbooks. But when the economy cooled off, services became less affordable and the gaps in our education became even more glaring. Dad had known how to unclog a sink. You hope you can remember the plumber's number and persuade him to come on a Sunday—and can float a loan to pay him. That's the bad news. The good news is that character may count for more than cash these days and resourcefulness may become the practical equivalent of money in the bank.

In the optimistic American way, we look on this present phase of ignorance as an opportunity—a steamer trunk of lost arts waiting to be opened. There's a long tradition in this country of believing one can improve oneself and in so doing, one's lot. These times and the book you hold in your hand will enable you to do just that. The ability to say please and thank you and smile politely is all very well, but it won't make for a very interesting life. Or help you when you need to iron a shirt or propose a toast. Your parents or a Significant Other may love you for who you are. But at any distance from their fond regard, it's not enough to merely *be*: you should be able to *do* a few things, too. This book will not give you a more powerful vocabulary or a dress code to triumph over the dictates of fashion. Your game of golf will not improve. However, follow its careful instructions and you'll be able to solve a good number of perplexing problems and save a variety of social situations. As important, with practice, this primer will allow you to amaze your friends and confound the dubious as they watch you, time and again, rising to the occasion.

HOW TO DANCE THE WALTZ

❖

Who needs to know how to waltz? That's like asking: Who needs romance? Who needs food and water? More times than you might imagine, the opportunity to dance will arise. Wedding receptions spring immediately to mind, and if you are the father of the bride, the mother of the groom, the bride, the groom, or a member of the wedding party, tradition holds a place for you on the dance floor. Less obvious, but more frequent, are the quiet Saturday evenings spent at home. Instead of selecting the channel with back-to-back sitcoms, you could blow the dust off an album with cheek-to-cheek potential and dance the night away. Somewhere in between once in a lifetime and once a week, there will be moments when knowing how to waltz will turn what looked like just another notation on your calendar into a memorable event.

Beyond social etiquette, and the possibility of salvaging an otherwise boring date, there is an added bonus in acquiring this skill. When you are dancing with a partner (who also knows how to dance), the music and its rhythm will allow you to transcend your daily woes.

You can start out with an imaginary partner (a broom

or thin air will do), but at some point you should try to find a real, live partner. While you are in the early stages of learning, rent a few Fred Astaire/Ginger Rogers movies just to get an idea of how the waltz is really done. The first thing you will notice is how effortless it seems to be, and then, if you are shy, you may notice that the two dancers appear to be attached at the waist. Years of practice will get you closer to the effortless stage. Simply standing closer to your partner will help in the meantime. It is always the hope that you enjoy your partner's company. However, if it is a "duty dance" (with portly Uncle Rosco or icky Cousin Cecile), or you are genuinely afraid of giving the wrong signal, arm's length is

perfectly acceptable. It just means the dancing will have to rely on two separate interpretations of the step (and the music) rather than a collaboration.

The leader's left hand extends out to the side and up just above shoulder height, and the right hand is placed lightly on the partner's back, fitting along the curve of the waist. The partner's right hand extends up and to the right, resting it in the hand of the leader, and the left hand should rest gently on the leader's right shoulder. (Surely this is a position you have seen many times in movies, plays, advertisements . . . relax, it's not difficult.) Your hands are placed in such a way so that you can signal to your partner should a careless couple come careening in your direction. A quick squeeze or tap will alert your unsuspecting partner, and suggest that the next step should be made with caution (probably in the opposite direction).

Traditionally, ballroom etiquette awards the "lead" to the male. If you have problems with this ruling, discuss it with your partner (be sure to include issues of skill, coordination, height, strength—but don't waste the entire evening on this point—maybe it's yours for the first dance, and your partner's for the second dance—just work it out). You may leave the matter open for a vote, draw straws, or decide that two modern day, rational, and equal partners will yield to tradition. However you decide to do it, one or the other of you must take the lead, otherwise you will be turning to the left, your partner will be heading off to the right, and all twenty toes will be stepped on before the dance is over. The lead dancer (think of Fred Astaire) tries to keep an eye on the dance-floor traffic (hence the motion is generally forward) while the partner (think of Ginger Rogers) watches for any attack from the rear. As Texas governor Ann Richards said, "She is doing everything Fred is doing, only backwards, and in high heels."

Having assumed the "ballroom" position . . . listen to the music. In order to waltz, there must be three beats per measure. You probably won't be looking at the score,

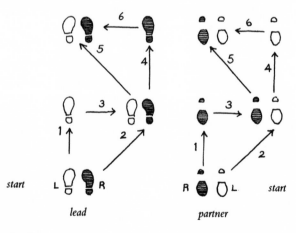

fig. 1

so you will have to rely on your ear and sense of rhythm (or the bandleader's announcement). Try to think of the three beats as being equal in time, but the first beat has a stronger accent. It sounds like "ONE, two, three, ONE, two, three, ONE, two, three." Once you have identified the rhythm, take the first step on the first, or strongest, beat. If it helps, replace "ONE, two, three; ONE, two, three" with "LEFT, right, left; RIGHT, left, right"— you don't have to say it out loud, but you may want to repeat it over and over to yourself, at least at first.

Look at the footprints on these pages. They should give you some indication of how these steps fit together. Your weight shifts naturally from right to left, and back to right. Three steps complete half of the pattern. Again,

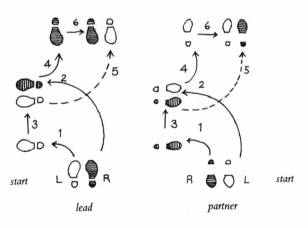

start   *lead*   *partner*   start

fig. 2

"LEFT, right, left" is followed by "RIGHT, left, right." These are not large steps, really not more than a foot. In fact, the smaller they are, the more control you will maintain (and your partner will have a much easier time keeping up with you). Speaking of your partner, remember, the leader is following the footprints (south to north), while the partner's back is to the north, and all the footwork is in reverse.

Figure 1 shows how to do the step in a relatively straight line. Once you feel comfortable with this approach, try turning as illustrated in Figure 2. Think of it as facing each other while standing on a swing. The leader goes forward with the first series of steps and backward for the second series—the partner correspondingly takes the first series backward and the second, forward. Both of you pivot slightly to the right or left depending upon the leader's pleasure, the contours of the room, or the other dancers on the floor.

Practice does make perfect. And believe it or not, practicing dancing can be almost as much fun as polished dancing. Listen to the music, engage in the rhythm, look deeply into your partner's eyes, and glide gently into the night.

HOW TO OPEN
A BOTTLE OF CHAMPAGNE

❖

According to the National Safety Council, someone is injured in the American home every nine seconds; every twenty-three minutes, one of these accidents is fatal. No statistics are available on the number of people disabled or felled for good by shooting champagne corks. Champagne corks may seem to constitute less of a threat than handguns or stepladders, but who wants to end up as a statistic, especially a small, silly one? Learn to open a bottle of champagne correctly and you're that much less likely to figure in the NSC's annual report.

Banish from your mind the scenes of locker-room bliss you've seen on television every time a baseball team wins a pennant. Those guys are more interested in wearing the Moët & Chandon than drinking it. For their purposes, a lesser brand would do just as well. (As would Dr Pepper or club soda.) However, as champagne is the drink as well as the bath of celebration, and bottles aren't sold with a user's guide, you had best study the following instructions.

Tear off the foil that covers the cork. Untwist the wire restraint that secured the cork during the fermentation.

In an ideal world, no one will have been using the bottle you're about to open as an Indian club in the past sixty minutes. Instead, the bottle will have been chilling primly on its side in the refrigerator or, if you were in a hurry and grabbed it from the vintner's shelf an hour before you intended to serve it, immersed in an ice bath to which you've added two to four tablespoons of salt (to accelerate the chilling process). Twenty minutes is all it will take to lower the bottle's temperature to a drinkable 45° to 48°. If you're the prudent sort, you may want to swathe the bottle's neck and cork in a dish towel or linen napkin and have a glass at the ready. (In the event that the bottle's contents are a little more agitated than you'd thought, the cloth will check the cork's propulsion across the room.) Angle the bottle away from you (and from any onlookers), grip the cork firmly with the towel or napkin, and begin to twist the cork. It should be a bit stiff. If the bottle has just come from the ice bath or the fridge, it may be slippery. Again, the towel will help you to get a grip. Twist the cork some more or turn the base of the bottle while holding onto the cork. Ease the cork out. You'll hear a satisfying little pop—not the cannon shot willfully produced by revelers less skilled than yourself—and then see a puff of carbonated white smoke, followed in even shorter order, once you tilt the bottle, by a

champagne flute

better for fruit cup

mass of delicious golden foam. This is why you had a champagne glass or two close at hand.

What's a champagne glass, you ask? We're told that the British like to drink champagne out of silver tankards. We know that caterers like to rent you glasses more appropriate to small shrimp cocktails or fruit cups. It's democratic but inaccurate to say that it doesn't really matter and that anything will do. If you go that route, a Dixie cup could be said to be just as good as a tall, narrow champagne flute. We can't agree. The flute's superiority is not arbitrary custom: its narrowness enhances the wine's aroma, its depth holds the bubbles just that much longer.

Is your mind's eye still averted from memories of locker-room bubble baths? Good. In serving champagne, you don't want to waste those precious bubbles and you don't want to hand your friends and relations glasses full of suds. So rather than holding the bottle aloft and making its contents dive from the height of your extended arm for the bottom of the glass, tilt the glass slightly and pour the champagne gently down its side. If you give your wrist a quarter twist just as you finish pouring, you will avoid dripping onto the carpet or the hand, sleeve, or lap of whomever you are serving. You might even consider wrapping the neck of the bottle in a napkin to forestall drips—not, of course, that a few drops of champagne ever ruined anything. (Avoiding drips is more important when pouring red wine, which leaves stains likely to annoy the house-proud.) But if you're going to be pouring six glasses immediately and then—second bottle, this is going to be some party—six more, your hand could always tremble. And remember the old sexist saw: "One takes a woman by the waist, a bottle by the neck."

You can avoid the trembling hand and the wasted champagne by using two hands. But this will look silly on a standard 750 milliliter bottle. A magnum—two bottles— or a jeroboam—four bottles—or even a Methuselah— eight bottles—would surely justify the use of two hands. The Salmanazar and the Nebuchadnezzar (twelve and twenty bottles, respectively) may call for a crane.

And remember, unless the champagne is cheap or sweet or, the worst of all worlds, both, you don't want it to be excessively cold. The colder it is, the less you'll taste it. If you're celebrating, don't you want as many senses intact as possible? Champagne is an excellent test of how many of those senses are functioning—as you lift the glass to your lips, you catch the wine's pleasant bouquet; the bubbles tickle your nose and, with the first sip, your palate. You watch the bubbles stream lazily but steadily to the top of your glass. Lift your glass for a toast and catch the light in its sparkling, albeit shallow depths.

HOW TO ARRANGE
FRESH FLOWERS

❖

I n some cultures, flower arranging is considered an art. Ours is not one of them. Sticking flowers into water when they arrive and throwing them out when they begin to droop or turn black is as high as some of us set our sights. Flowers are classed with goldfish, except that they require less attention. There are even a few hard-eyed individuals ready to resist both the beauty and pleasure flowers bring with the hollow, high-minded disclaimer, "What's the point? They're only going to die." With an attitude like that no birthday cake would ever get decorated and no one would ever iron a shirt. Or make a bed for that matter. Life is not long enough for such shortsighted foolishness. Are we to dislike kittens because they only turn into cats and baby's smiles because, soon enough, they'll need braces? Of course not. We can take heart from the fact that doing something attractive with fresh flowers is a less long-term commitment than child or cat care.

Luckily, in the fresh-flower department, you don't need a green thumb, or a climate like California's, because flowers are available year round—at a stand next to the subway entrance, at the supermarket, the farmers' market, and, for a little bit more money, at your local florist. There can be tulips in January just as easily as there is holly in December.

Let's say the new couple you had to dinner last weekend has had the unforgettably good idea of sending flowers or, you, thinking there must be some cheap cure for a rainy Saturday afternoon in March, have bought yourself a dozen tulips. Now what? All you need is a little thought, a little time, and a little equipment. Actually, all you really need is a container of water and the flowers.

If you have Oasis (a block of solidified green plastic

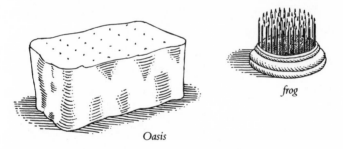

frog

Oasis

foam, available at your city's answer to the five-and-dime) or a "frog" (a heavy, metal cylinder composed of closely set, needlelike prongs on a flat base), or a nylon net bag containing clear marbles, you will have an easier time making the flowers stand or lean at the desired angle. No frogs available? Try putting the greens (fern or laurel, whatever the vendor has on hand to match the type of flower you buy) into the vase first in a crisscross pattern. Then put the flowers in, one at a time, resting them against the structure provided by the greens. If there are no greens, you may have luck with a rubber band or piece of thread wrapped around the gathered stems. Do not rely on the leaves still attached to the flowers' stems for propping. Leaves below the waterline should be removed beforehand, otherwise they rapidly decay, spoiling the water in the vase and accelerating the deterioration of your arrangement.

Wash the vase thoroughly. It may have been collecting dust (or holding remnants from the last bunch of flowers) and be in need of a good scrub. Choose one that has a small neck, particularly if you do not have any Oasis. The narrow neck averts the jackstraws look. If preference or necessity is going to place your bouquet in a basket or a bowl, a small juice glass or an olive jar filled with water placed in the center of the container will hold the flower stems in some kind of order. Extra greens around the base will provide camouflage for the underpinnings.

Where are you going to put this cheery bunch of zinnias? In the center of the dining-room table? In the living room, guest room, on your desk? You need to think about height and shape. You don't want to hold a dinner conversation through a bank of iris, nor do you want to give the blossomless backside of a daffodil spray to the other half of the office pool. If the arrangement will be seen from all angles, you should plan to follow a spherical shape. If there is to be a backside, you can form a triangle, semicircle or tiered affair. Daring sorts may experiment with the asymmetrical (and of course you can claim that was just what you were hoping to achieve should yours turn out to fit that description).

Odd numbers of flowers sharing shape and color lend some order, or balance, to the grouping. For instance, three red roses alternated with three marguerite daisies will be complemented by five stalks of deep blue larkspur. Colors should be considered both in terms of where the flowers will be (what colors are in the guest room or the tablecloth), and the combination of secondary and primary colors. Blues, reds, and purples work well together, but don't add yellow or orange to the group unless you are going for the whole-garden look. Two primaries and any number of secondaries derived from those primaries is an easy rule of thumb. If this seems too complicated, stick with a single color and a variety of flowers. Don't know what the room looks like? Can't remember which tablecloth is clean? A vase of daisies and baby's breath (basic white on white) is pretty anywhere.

Back to the arrangement. While you are deciding on the height, shape, and color, the flowers should be in a container of fresh water. If these flowers are straight from the garden, they should be given several hours (some say overnight) in the bucket to adjust. Lupine, which gracefully bows down, will curl up; daylily blossoms will close; rosebuds may open. Always check the stems to be sure they are strong and healthy. All stems, damaged or healthy, need to be trimmed. A diagonal cut will expose more surface area and increase the flow of water to the leaves and blossoms. In fact, you can increase the lifetime of a bouquet by replacing two-day-old water with fresh water and giving the stems a second trim. Stems that have been pinched or bent will not be able to transport water to the blossom, and within six hours your carefully arranged bouquet will look as if a delivery truck backed over it. To avoid this early demise, trim any damaged stems just above the point of break or bruise. If the trimming is severe, the original plan for size and style of arrangement may have to be altered. For instance, if the break is just below the blossom, and the blossom is one of three in the arrangement, consider floating all three in a shallow bowl.

Now, with vase, water, flowers of the right height and color, greens or filler (baby's breath, dusty miller, Queen Anne's lace), it's assembly time. Start with the greens, covering the rim of the vase (hiding the Oasis or frog), building toward the center to form the basic shape chosen for the arrangement (fig. 1). Take three blossoms of the same color and shape, they will form the first triangle to be nestled in the greens (fig. 2). Depending on the number of blossoms, their colors, and sizes, you can build on the first triangle by clustering each point (fig. 3).

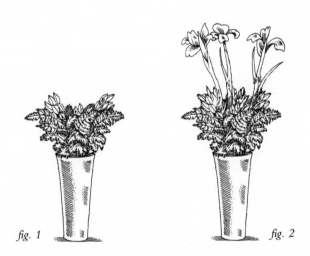

fig. 1

fig. 2

For example, the three irises with twelve-inch stems form a seven-inch equilateral triangle; each iris can be accompanied by a white columbine, a lavender columbine, and two bunches of honeysuckle. As long as you match the three points with each addition, your arrangement will be artfully balanced with the single addition of a center, usually a fourth blossom of the most dominant (or interesting) group—in this case the iris (fig. 4). You may not like your first effort. Take everything out and try again. Many a perfect arrangement has survived four or five false beginnings.

Sounds a little too controlled? You only had enough

fig. 3

cash for what now seems like a boring bunch of yellow mums? Follow along as far as the clean vase/clipped stems advice, and then try letting them fall as they please. You probably shouldn't plan on this technique for centerpiece quality. At the same time, you probably can count on a punctual guest to worry over them (the very same guest who attacks the crooked bow tie or the poorly laid fire—most likely to be firstborn, the victim of early potty training). Regardless of shape and color scheme, or the amount of time and talent required, an arrangement of fresh flowers can begin to turn your gloomy Saturday afternoon into a gala Saturday evening.

fig. 4

HOW TO TIE A BOW TIE

❖

Dressed in an evening gown, the woman is putting on her earrings or applying the last touches to her make-up. The man is wearing black trousers, white braces, and a white formal shirt. "Darling," he says, "can you help me with this?" "This," of course, is his bow tie and, without his "darling," he's lost.

In classic American movies and, perhaps, in our parents' bedrooms, we've watched this scene many times. Life imitates the movies and the routine act of tying a bow tie is believed to be an arcane skill on the order of a Greg Louganis dive, well beyond the reach of the merely coordinated. It isn't. It's only slightly different from, and not much harder than, tying your shoe—something that you probably learned to do when you were five years old—provided you turned six before Velcro flaps replaced laces. You're more advanced in eye-hand coordination than you were then. Now you have years of shaving without removing your nose to your credit. So step up to the mirror and try this out.

For the sake of practice, cut the letters A and B from a magazine and tape each to an end of your practice tie—not the Italian silk. Adjust the band of the tie to match your neck size. Unless your tie is very old, very expensive, or custom-made, it will probably adjust to several different sizes. Fit the band under your collar, fold the collar back down, and let the two ends of the tie hang down your shirtfront with the end on your left, let's say A, falling about 1.5" short of B (fig. 1). Don't bother with a tape measure. A should come to the hourglass waist of B.

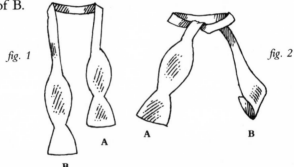

fig. 1

fig. 2

Now, take A in your left hand, cross it over, under, up, and over the long end (B), pulling both ends until the tie is snuggish but not strangling. A now dangles over B, with its end trailing just to the waist of B (fig. 2).

Form the front loop of the bow by holding A at the point where it curves in—the hourglass waist—and then doubling it up toward your chin with your index and middle fingers and your thumbs (fig. 3). Pinching the folded fabric at the midpoint, give it a quarter turn so

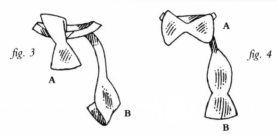

fig. 3

A

B

fig. 4

A

B

that the right half of the bow is now horizontal, lying over your right collar point (fig. 4).

Next, take the band of B with your right hand and draw it up over the fingers with which you are pinching the A half of the bow and then down behind, between the left thumbnail and the tie band on which it rests (fig. 5).

Push the broad part of B through the back of the loop that has just been formed, pushing toward the left (fig. 6). You'll want to help it through with your right index finger, evening up the bow you have just tied and tightening it in such a way that the whole arrangement lies more or less flat and more or less horizontal (fig. 7). It should look as if a rather portly butterfly has just made a three-point landing on your collar button (fig. 8). Unless you want it to look like the badly tied gift bow on a

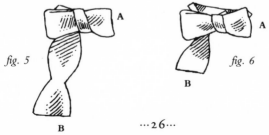

fig. 5

A

B

B

fig. 6

A

B

hastily wrapped package or an airplane propeller halted in midspin, you need to work on it a bit. A rakish tilt to your tie will only encourage others to fuss with it. Unless you want this sort of attention, better fix it yourself.

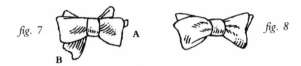

fig. 7   A   B   *fig. 8*

"Why," you may wonder, "do I need to go to the trouble of tying my own bow tie when clip-ons are available?" Or the kind that, rather than clipping directly to the collar, hooks under the collar at the back of your neck. "I had one when I was ten and it worked all right." Because, like a bad wig or the smile on a corpse, such a bow tie looks too neat, too perfect. It's like artificial flowers or the plastic sushi some Japanese restaurants display in their windows.

Anyone can tie a bow tie. Not everyone should wear one. If you have a heavy face, if you have no neck and you wear your hair very short, a bow tie may not be for you. If, on the other hand, you're feeling free spirited and hearty enough to weather the mix of ridicule and admiration from the office crew, perfect that knot and wear it with pride.

HOW TO CHANGE A FUSE

❖

Let's get one thing straight about magical thought: Thinking about something bad happening—getting a run in your stocking, getting a flat tire, blowing a fuse—won't make it happen. By the same token, shooing your mind away from undesirable outcomes doesn't necessarily prevent them. If you say, for example, "I guess I shouldn't plug in the iron and run the blender at the same time," and then ignore your own better judgment, you don't get credit for sort of knowing you were doing the wrong thing. Hoping for the best doesn't change the load on the electrical circuit one ampere.

Imagination is not nearly as effective a teacher as experience, but one of its slight pedagogical virtues is that it subjects the student to less inconvenience. So let's imagine that you, the student of fuse-changing, are alone in your apartment, making efficient use of your free time. Better yet, let's imagine you're alone in your borrowed or sublet apartment, identically employed. Night has fallen, the news is over, and you've washed your supper dishes. You're not zoned out in front of the television, you're not listening to an inarticulate friend ramble on about his goals in life on the telephone, you're not dancing buck naked in front of the pier glass with the stereo turned way up. It was time to turn over a new leaf and that's what you've done. Your printer is printing out the second draft of a long report you've been working on. The countertop rotisserie is turning and basting the chicken you intend to serve yourself for the next week and the mini washer-dryer unit your host was just able to fit into an underutilized corner of the apartment and about which he told you something that has slipped your mind is gently thumping away in the background.

"What the heck," you say to yourself, setting up the ironing board, "may as well turn on the iron while I'm at it." You find the last remaining socket amid the viperlike tangle of cords sprouting from the extender unit stuck into the wall socket, shove the plug into it, and turn on the iron.

You hadn't realized how noisy it was until all noise ceases. All at once. The dryer shuts off. The rotisserie neither turns nor bastes. Your report ceases to print. Even the gooseneck lamp you had jerryrigged to give you a little more light in that cell of a kitchen goes out. Fade, no, cut to black.

"Hmmm," you say to yourself, shushing the voice of conscience, "it's probably a general power failure." You can still hear the neighbor's television. Perhaps it's one of those battery-powered TVs so many people have, you reflect, moving to the window. The street has not gone dark. You hear no sirens. The inconsiderate neighbors on the other side seem to have a battery-powered television, too. Perhaps the power failure isn't all that general after all. To gain a little time before facing the inevitable, you review other possibilities. A burnt-out bulb in the gooseneck wouldn't shut off the dryer, would it? Might an overbasted chicken have an effect on the printer? Probably not, unless the wires were very seriously crossed. No, it's just as you feared, you've blown a fuse. The apartment being borrowed, this is indeed a worst-case scenario.

Locate the fuse box and remember what you learned in junior high science: Electricity is a current flowing through conductors. In order to flow, the current must have an unimpeded path from start to finish, from source of power through some device using electricity such as a light bulb or a washer-dryer and back to its source. Fuses and circuit breakers protect electrical systems from damage caused by too much current passing through them. This excess of current can be caused by a sudden surge from the power company, too many appliances plugged into one circuit, or some problem with your system. If that happens, the fuse blows or the circuit breaker is tripped and the supply of electricity is cut off.

This is a good thing. A nuisance, perhaps, but a good thing. The alternatives are all much less convenient and one of them involves the fire department. Open the fuse box and look inside. It may contain fuses or, if the building is of recent construction or its wiring has been redone in the past twenty or thirty years, circuit breakers. In which case you're not looking in a fuse box at all. Call it a service panel. But the principle remains the same. If there's been an overload or a short circuit, a fuse will have blown or a circuit breaker will have tripped. How can you tell what's what?

Fuses come in several types, circuit breakers in one. A circuit breaker looks like a light switch and serves both as a switch and a fuse. As a switch, it lets you open a circuit by toggling to OFF if you want to work on the wiring. Not your problem. (If you want to make it your problem, you'll want more thorough guidance than this chapter provides.) As a fuse, it provides the same automatic overcurrent protection that real fuses do. If the circuit breaker has been tripped by an overload, the switch flips to OFF. Unplug the last thing you turned on and throw the circuit breaker to ON or RESET.

Plug or type **S** fuses have bases similar to ordinary light bulbs and are rated up to thirty amperes. Generally speaking, the higher the number the bigger the appliance—clothes dryers get thirty, table lamps get ten. The metal strip you see through the glass head is a link in the electric circuit. If the amperage flowing into the circuit exceeds that for which the fuse is rated, this metal strip will break or melt. If the fuse blows because of a short-circuit, the window will usually be blackened or discolored. If an overload is responsible, the strip will be broken. Fusetron or time-delay fuses permit a momentary overload and are used mainly on circuits for major appliances such as ovens and washers and large power tools. A type S fuse, now required in all new installations, cannot be screwed into a fuse socket if an adapter with the correct rating has not been screwed in first. With the older type of fuse, you have to be careful not to replace it with one of higher amperage. The type S fuse makes such a mistake impossible.

plug fuse   *fusetron fuse*   *type S fuse*

cartridge or
ferrule-type fuse

A cartridge fuse, on the other hand, is a round cylinder shaped like a piece of chalk or the tip of an umbrella or a cane, which is why it's also called a ferrule-type fuse. It's rated from ten to sixty amps and is generally used to protect the circuit of an individual appliance. Housed in a fuse holder, this housing pulls straight out from the service panel. A special tool may be required to separate fuse and fuse holder. As is the case with plug fuses, cartridge fuses must be replaced with fuses of the same amperage. Were you to replace it with one rated higher, you'd be defeating the whole purpose of having overcurrent protection. Whichever kind of fuse you're using, it's good to have spares on hand.

After shutting off the main switch—at the top of the box—remove the blown fuse by turning it counterclockwise. If you, or the person who rents the apartment, had the presence of mind the last time this happened to buy two or three new fuses just in case and to store them within plain sight of the fuse box, your problems are probably over.

Obviously, it will do no real good to replace a fuse or reset the circuit breaker until you've figured out why it blew in the first place. An overloaded circuit is often the problem. Unplug the iron and the gooseneck lamp. Turn everything else off, too. Now replace the blown fuse, taking care to grasp the fuse only by its outer glass rim. Also, don't be standing in a puddle of water as you do this. (You get out of the lake when lightning flickers on the horizon, don't you?) If the fuse box happens to be in a damp basement, put down a dry board to stand on. Reduce your chances of forming a complete circuit by replacing the fuse with one hand only. Keep your free hand behind you or in your pocket, or use it to hold a flashlight, if the darkness is general.

If this solves the problem, your chicken will start to roast again and your clothes to dry but the ironing will remain undone. Wait until the chicken is done, or plug the iron into an outlet on another circuit and carry on.

If putting in a new fuse and decreasing the number of appliances plugged into that one circuit doesn't fix the problem, you may have a short circuit somewhere. The blackened window of the blown fuse is a tip-off. Most short circuits occur in flexible cords, plugs, or appliances. Black smudge marks on the outlet or frayed or charred cords are indicators. Replace the damaged cord or plug before wasting a new fuse or resetting the breaker.

What do you do if you don't have spare fuses? What you *don't* do is reestablish the circuit by inserting a penny at the base of the fuse socket. Is there an all-night hardware store in your neighborhood? No? Since guests aren't due in half an hour, everything is cool. You've got a half-roasted fowl, a half-printed report, and three unironed shirts. The half-dried laundry will dry itself just the way it used to—over the shower rack. The fowl can be put in the fridge and the report on the back burner. Tomorrow is another day and the hardware store will be open. Go to bed and read a book. If the whole place is dark, go to bed and read a book by flashlight.

But, alternate reality, perhaps life is such that you must get that bird basted, must get that Santa Claus suit completely dry, and the report won't wait. Now's the time to go see the man upstairs or the woman next door—you did remember to return the cup of sugar or the half-dozen eggs you borrowed, didn't you? You didn't have to be asked a second time to turn down the stereo, did you?—and see if they have a fuse you could borrow. And if they don't and you're both good neighbors, perhaps they'll let you use their oven to finish the chicken.

HOW TO
CHANGE A FLAT TIRE

❖

Suppose you haven't joined Triple A, the last phone booth you noticed was at a roadside stand forty-five minutes ago, and because of the way the car has begun pulling toward the cornfield on the right, you think you may have a flat tire. Slow down, put on your blinker, and look for a wide shoulder along a straightway (curves and hills tend to obscure the vision of oncoming overloaded log trucks). Pull over and put on the emergency brake. We've known plenty of respectable people who have driven cars that may not pass the next inspection because of a failing emergency brake. It's not a social flaw. But if you find that the tire *is* flat, and you are the only one around to change it, an emergency brake comes in handy. A big rock or log or something under the tire that will bear the most weight should perform the same duty. The idea is to keep the car stationary while it's being tilted by the jack.

The jack? It's probably in the trunk of your car. Read your owner's manual. Third owner? Borrowed car? "I don't think this car came with a manual . . ." Look underneath and/or around the spare tire. Yes, you'll probably have to unpack most of your belongings. Try to keep the cat in the front seat. There may be a small case of tools (including a socket wrench and screwdriver), and a cylindrical affair with a handle. That's the jack. Next, hope that your spare tire is fully inflated as you haul it out of the trunk. Lean it against the car near the tire you're going to replace. Go back and get the jack and tools. Pry the hubcap off of the flat with the screwdriver (fig. 1). Loosen the nuts with a socket wrench or tire iron (fig. 2), using a counterclockwise motion. Sometimes it is easier to loosen them alternately, that is, loosen #1, skip to #3, then to #4 and down to #2.

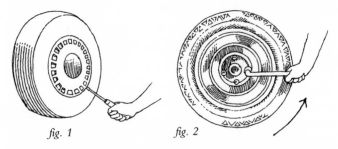

fig. 1   *fig. 2*

There are two critical moments in tire changing. The second is when the spare turns out to be sound, the first is when you have located the spot where the jack should meet the frame of the car. You won't know about the second until you have completed the job. You won't know about the first until you have knelt, scooched, crawled, or wriggled to get underneath the car well enough to see what's what. On some (foreign) cars, there may be an eye or slot on the frame made especially for the corresponding piece at the end of the jack's stiff arm. Slot or no slot, you want the body of the jack to meet the frame (not the body, it crumples) of the car, and it should be as close to the flat tire as possible. Of course the jack may need to be adjusted in order to fit under the car. Take your time, fool around with it, figure out what makes it go up and down. You've got all day. It's not going exactly according to plan, so why not relax and be entertained by what you would have missed if it had.

Now that you've found the where and how, jack up the car and remove the nuts you have already loosened on the flat, putting them thoughtfully inside the hubcap that is lying next to you. Take off the flat. Put on the spare. Replace the nuts in the same alternating pattern. Jack the car down. Say a quick prayer. If the spare is holding air, tighten the nuts—use as much strength as you have. Then tap the hubcap back into place, put the flat and all the tools you were able to find back into the trunk. Reload the rest of your belongings, brush off your hands and knees, and admire your work. Not bad for a first try.

— Again, the simple procedure described above assumes the ideal flat tire on a deserted country road on a bright, sunny day. What if your spare is flat? What if it's the middle of the night during a freezing rainstorm? What if you can't get the nuts off because you can't find any tools? That's when the operative phrase begins with "discretion" and ends with "valor." Meaning it's all very well to be brave but you don't have to be foolish, too. Tying a white handkerchief to the car door or antenna attracts attention, putting the hood up adds twenty points . . . holding the cat as you lean against the right side of the disabled vehicle will give you a 98 percent chance of bringing out the best in the next passing Good Samaritan. Sometimes rising to the occasion involves graciously accepting help when it is obviously needed.

HOW TO
JUMP-START A CAR

❖

Congratulations. You've landed a terrific job, with all sorts of opportunity for advancement and networking. The work is definitely interesting, your co-workers are young and enthusiastic. You've just signed your first lease for a summer cottage on the lake. The phone is installed. The U-Haul is packed. And Grandfather has been more than generous, taking his prize 1963 VW black beetle off the blocks and presenting it to you with a modest, "How else would you get to the office on time?" Life is full of promise. Well, pretty full. The work is every bit as interesting as you had anticipated, the co-workers (one in particular) are a great bunch, the kerosene heater does a reasonable job of keeping the cottage above freezing. But every now and again, Gramps's question comes back to haunt you. It's not the alarm clock that doesn't go off, it's not the hot water that doesn't go on, it's the engine that doesn't turn over that keeps you from getting to the office on time. Security deposits, installation fees, and the office birthday fund have cleaned out two advances and any hope of getting to a garage. Time to learn how to jump-start a car.

Ignore the option of calling a wrecker—if you had enough money to pay the auto association's membership fee, you could probably afford to leave the car at the shop for an afternoon. This is advice for one who is two weeks from payday with a roommate who works the night shift in the newsroom. Or for one of two who have enjoyed a breakfast cooked on the open fire, folded up the tent, and checked the map for the most scenic route to today's destination. It is advice for anyone who knows the heart-sinking feeling that comes with a turn of the key followed by silence. Jumper cables should be in the trunk of every car, particularly every used, borrowed, elderly, unfamiliar car. Even if you drive a brand new car, jumper cables in the trunk are like Clark Kent in a phone booth. Regardless of who is in distress, with this set of wires and clamps and some idea of how to use them, you can be the one to save the day.

So, open the hood of your car (there may be a lever inside, somewhere under the dashboard near the steering wheel, helpfully labelled HOOD RELEASE). Otherwise it's just a latch under the center point of the hood. Lift the hood—it's not heavy—and look for the metal rod that rests along the edge of the frame just under the hood. Some models claim to automatically prop open (and stay open). Most older models don't. So, pull the rod up and stick its end into the matching hole in the underside of the hood. That will keep the hood from crashing down on your back. If you can't find the rod, and you are doing this by yourself, look around for a substitute—a broom, a shovel, a ski pole, or hockey stick—use your imagination. A hood that has been properly propped open allows you to actually work on the engine *and* attract motoring do-gooders. Both features are essential to successful jump-starting because the cables only work when they are connecting your tired-out battery to one that is up and running. Without your roommate's truck, the neighbor's car, or the heaven-sent motorist who just happened by in a sporty red roadster, your cables are nothing more than an unwieldy jump rope.

A few more serious words of caution: Turn off the engine of the car (the one that works). Put out your cigarettes. Tuck in shirttails, flowing tresses, anything that could get caught up in the machinery and take you with it.

The hood is up on your sleeping beauty. The vehicle of mercy, jaw similarly agape, has snuggled up alongside whichever side will put the two batteries closest together *without* touching . . . otherwise known as the first date position. It is very important to be sure that the only points of contact between the two vehicles are the cables. (Note: The battery, usually black in color, is a deep box with plastic caps and two metal heads on top. "Maintenance free" batteries do not have plastic caps covering the water cells—there are no water cells. Standard batteries do and these cells should be checked (just pry off the cap and look inside) for water before you try to give it a charge. If they are empty, fill them up. One head, the red one, is marked with a + for positive; the other head, the black one, is marked - for negative. Once you can identify the battery and its parts, you will have a better chance of finding it—locations vary as much as make and model.)

Now, with engines off and emergency brakes on, it is time to connect the batteries—in this order: First, clamp the red cable to the positive head of the dead battery, then clamp the other end of the red cable to the positive head of the live battery. Next clamp the black cable to the negative head of the live battery and the other end of the black cable to the unpainted frame of the car (which serves nicely as a "ground"), *not* to the negative head of the dead battery, otherwise sparks may occur, igniting gasses that may surround the battery. Got that? So it's red for me, red for you, then black for you, and ground for me.

Cables in place? Okay, the driver of the car that started up this morning, fire your engines. Actually, just turn the car on, and gently rev the engine, not to put it

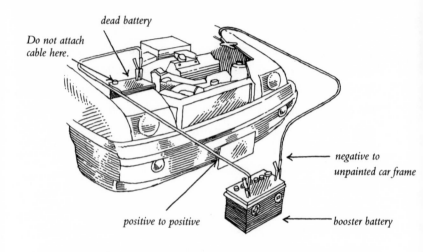

dead battery

Do not attach
cable here.

negative to
unpainted car frame

booster battery

positive to positive

through the hood, but to transfer a little juice. Driver of
the car that didn't start up this morning, turn your key.
No point in running the radio, air conditioner, and
headlights right now, so why not turn them off until the
battery has a chance to build up a little juice of its own?
Once both engines are running—don't turn them off—
remove the cables in the reverse order. So, that would be
ground for me, black for you, red for you, red for me.
Right? Time to put the hood down. Do make sure the
latch has caught. See what you can do to remove the
grease and grime before you shake hands with the noble
soul who stopped to help. Put the cables back into the

trunk, take a deep breath, and prepare yourself for the rest of the day.

Preparation should include driving around for some time in an effort to charge up the battery. If your infinite wisdom tells you that the judge will not grant that request for delay, drive to the filling station nearest the office, and ask them to charge your battery for you. Unless the battery is recharged, either by driving around or by a transfusion, you will be repeating this exercise when the workday ends.

There is a second method of jump-starting. It was more prevalent in earlier years, before automatic transmissions and catalytic converters, but in special circumstances, it is still effective. We return to the 1963 VW your grandfather generously bestowed upon you, the perfect subject for this second method because it has a standard transmission and there is no computerized or electronic device to trigger the ignition. It's the car for Luddites who live outside the loop of public transportation. They can think of starting the car in the way they think of starting a fire. All you need is a gradual grade for one and two rocks for the other. If your car does not fit the above description, do not try this method—it won't work. What's worse, it can easily turn a frustration into a disaster. Modern steering wheels have a tendency to lock in position, making the curve at the bottom of the hill nonnegotiable. If your car is young enough to have a catalytic converter, hill or push-starting can damage the mechanism (which costs more than the tow truck will charge for a single visit). Clearly stated—to avoid your disappointment and eliminate our liability, you can only try this trick on old cars.

Here's the scenario. You drive a funky old car. It has a name. You talk to it, coax it, listen to it. Every day you depend on it to get you to this fabulous new job and home again. One night Babs doesn't respond to the turn of your key, at least not right away as she always has. "Come on, Babsie, it's been a long day for both of us, and I really want to get home in time to see the playoffs." You sit, you wait, and three minutes later you give her another try. Ta daah! She turns over, you begin to smile, and together you ride into the sunset. Hold it, freeze frame . . . sure you're in a hurry, but that doesn't excuse you from the dynamics of the relationship. She is not a coy mistress, and to be honest, you probably don't have world enough or time. Unless you want to be high and dry tomorrow morning, you should take some precautionary steps. Ideally you live at the top of a knoll, or at the bottom of one, and in either case you have a long, straight driveway. If you fall shy of the ideal, try to think of a 200 to 300 yard stretch (within walking distance of your abode) that has a slight grade and little to no traffic. Asking for permission to park somewhere near the high point of this hill (don't turn off the engine when you go to ask, in case the answer is no) will keep your car from being towed at the neighbor's request and it may elicit an offer to give you a push in the morning.

All right, so dawn is breaking, and you awaken before the alarm with a surge of purpose. "Let's see if she starts." Babs tries, but each time you turn the key, her Rrraah-rrraahhrrrr becomes weaker. Time to take the neighbor up on that offer, and on your way to the door, what about a quick review of the actual procedure?

You're in the car. There is no traffic coming or going by. Your left foot is holding in the clutch, your right foot is holding the brake, the car is in first gear. Release the emergency brake, turn on the ignition, wave to signal preparation for lift off (or "push") as you take your right foot off the brake, keeping the left foot on the clutch. The car starts to roll. When you have picked up a jog-ger's pace (or if you have used up half the length of your runway) it's time to pop the clutch. Pow, pop, buck, and hey, there goes the engine. Put the clutch back in. You may have to use the heel of your right foot to brake while you give that baby some extra gas (really rev it up) for being so good. Of course, it may be pow, pop, and buck are followed by silence, in which case you still have the second half of the hill for another try. (Better be sure there's room for parking at the bottom, just in case Babs can't find it in her heart to rally.) Remember to drive around for a while, make it a celebratory tour of the city, to charge up the battery, and you might consider looking for a parking place that would allow for a repeat performance after work.

Like so many of life's challenges, practice makes for a near-perfect remedy, but most of us are hard-pressed to fake an emergency for the sake of rehearsal. Unlike many of the occasions addressed in this book—the clogged drain or the missing button spring to mind—hill-starting a car is not only impressive, but it's fun. So when co-workers start grousing about finely printed policies containing $1,000 deductibles for towing, you can stand a little taller, smile a little broader (send Grandfather an update on how you and Babs are getting along), and invite some of the uninitiated to join you for a demonstration in the EEE lot.

Note: Unless this lack of current is linked to a radio that was left to play all night, or a car door that didn't quite close enough to turn out the overhead lamp, you will tire rather quickly of either method. If the situation doesn't improve with a long drive, the dead battery may only be symptomatic of bigger trouble . . . the kind only your mechanic can adequately fix. Tolerance will decrease as occurrences increase, making the trade-off of no lunch for two weeks for an afternoon in the shop seem like a bargain.

HOW TO BOIL AN EGG
(with hints on further uses for boiled water)

❖

Boiling an egg is the simplest of tasks. Indeed, it is so simple that not knowing how to boil an egg is the standard calibration for zero on the scale of culinary sophistication. There are about as many ways to boil an egg as there are to skin a cat. They're all easier and considerably more in demand. Look in any cookbook. Better yet, look in several. Although there are plenty of variants—lid on, lid off, rolling boil, barely simmering, and so forth—all will produce edible cooked eggs. Here are a few methods:

First method: Put two eggs in a saucepan. Cover them with cold water. Bring the water to a boil on the top of your stove. Once the water is boiling, turn the burner down so that the water is just simmering. For soft-boiled eggs—runny yolks, barely set whites—remove them after they've simmered for two to three minutes. For medium-soft-boiled eggs—whites firm, yolks soft but not too runny—remove them after they've simmered for four minutes. Hard-boiled eggs can simmer for eight to

ten minutes, fifteen if you like them the consistency of golf balls.

Second method: Bring a quart of water to a boil in a fairly deep saucepan. Remove it from the burner and gently lower two eggs, one at a time, into the water with a tablespoon. *Gently.* (It's astounding but true that an uncooked egg, tossed from a second-story window onto a lawn, will not break. Equally astounding, equally true, is the fact that the same egg, clenched in a bodybuilder's iron fist, will not crack. However, the same is not true for two eggs, removed from the rack on the refrigerator door and rudely dropped into a rolling boil. So, don't bounce them.) Put a lid on the pan and return it to the burner to simmer. In four minutes, you will have a soft-boiled egg.

Third method: Bring a saucepan of water to a boil. Remove it from the heat and lower your two eggs into the pan. Cover it and return to the flame. Once the water boils again, allow three minutes for soft-boiled eggs, eight for hard boiled.

Fourth method: Bring a quart of water to a rolling boil. Lower two eggs into the water. Remove the pan from the heat, cover it, and let it sit for ten minutes. Your eggs will be somewhere between hard and soft-boiled—the whites well-set and the yolks soft but not runny.

Fifth method: plunge the eggs into boiling water. Cover and leave on the burner *one* minute. Remove pan from the burner and let it sit for five.

Somewhere among these five methods there should be a process and a product to suit nearly anyone's taste. The eggs plunged into already boiling water will have tougher whites, the whites of the eggs that started in cold water will be more tender. Also, eggs brought slowly to a boil are less likely to crack. Choose the cooking method that suits your temperament.

If you're not planning to eat the eggs immediately and just want to have some cold hard-boiled eggs around, start them in cold water—first method—turn off the stove after the water has returned to a boil, cover the pan, and let it all sit until the water has cooled down to lukewarm.

The final step is shelling the boiled eggs. Remove them from the water and immerse them in a cold water bath. After a minute, tap each egg on a hard surface to crack its shell or rap it all over with a knife handle to produce a network of cracks. If the egg is soft-boiled, you can scoop the contents out onto a piece of toast or set it upright in an egg cup, cut the top clean off, and eat your egg with a spoon right out of the shell. If the egg is hard-boiled, remove the shell and membrane and rinse the peeled egg under running water to get rid of any stray bits. Proceed with your breakfast, hors d'oeuvre, or physics experiment.

A couple of suggestions: Keeping the water at a simmer, or at most, a gentle boil means that you won't be driven mad by the sound of eggs rattling around the bottom of the pan, trying to get out, or equally annoying, bouncing into one another like bumper cars, thereby cracking their shells and releasing filaments of albumen into the water before their whites have set.

Cool the eggs quickly after boiling and you'll be spared the sight of an unappealing gray yolk. Quick cooling also makes the eggs easier to shell. So does shelling them when they're still slightly warm to the touch. But if you're not planning to use them right away, they'll have to go back into the refrigerator and you'll have to do your best with peeling them later on. If you want a real challenge, try boiling eggs you've just brought home from the market. If they're as fresh as you hope, the shell will be *impossible* to remove. The white will look as if it's been pecked by hens. If this isn't your idea of fun, buy the eggs you intend to hard cook two days in advance. Finally, if you're the cautious type and want to be sure the eggs don't crack while boiling, you can always make a hole with a thumbtack or a needle in the egg's fatter end before you put it into the water.

The only negative thing to say about boiled eggs is that you can't check their progress. Nature's much-touted perfect package frustrates that reassuring operation. But follow one of the above directions and your boiled egg will surely please someone.

Beyond eggs

Of course, eggs are not the only thing you can cook in boiling water. Potatoes, broccoli, Brussels sprouts, brisket of beef, an old hen—the list goes on and on but as this is not a cookbook we're not going to give you a single recipe. We will give you a tip, however. If you're just one step beyond not knowing how to cook an egg, you'll know enough to have a recipe and a vegetable in front of you just before you put the water on to boil. And after you've read a few recipes, you'll note with interest that root vegetables—carrots, parsnips, potatoes, and beets—are best started in cold water and brought to a boil (recall egg-boiling method number one), whereas green beans, peas, and so forth are plunged, briefly, into water that's already boiling. Or, better yet, they're steamed.

Of course, if you don't have any vegetables handy, you could always make yourself a pot of tea. It's cheap, it's comforting, and it won't add a calorie or a milligram of cholesterol to your daily intake.

Bring to a boil enough water to rinse out your teapot with an extra cupful. This removes dust, in the event that it's been a while since you've used it, and, more importantly, heats the pot. In the bottom of the scalded pot, place one teaspoon of loose tea per cup and one additional teaspoon "for the pot." If you don't like the idea of tea leaves floating around in your cup, you can put the tea in a tea ball, a ceramic or metal doodad shaped like a large acorn and equipped with a screw-on lid and pierced with lots of holes; you lower it into the teapot just before you fill the pot with water. Or, if this seems like a nuisance, you can use a strainer when pouring out the tea. Or, if you just want something hot and dark to drink, a teabag is the easiest of all.

for the teapot   *for the teacup*

Whether you confine the tea to a tea ball or not, under no circumstances should you leave the water boiling endlessly before you make the tea. Unless you're hiking in the mountains and are worried about *Giardia* or are getting your water from a roadside ditch and are just plain worried, you want the water hot, not purified. Boiling drives the oxygen out and makes for a flat-tasting cup of tea. So, when the water has just begun to boil, pour it into the pot, let the tea steep until it's the strength you like, and then pour yourself a cup.

As with boiled eggs, so with tea: *de gustibus non est disputandam.* The British serve a second pot of plain boiled water so the tea, once poured, can be diluted to each drinker's taste. And they put the milk in first. Further north, in the Western Isles of Scotland, tea is drunk strong. Ideally, a spoon will stand upright, unaided. South of the Sahara, "Arab tea" is drunk so strong and sweet the novice gets a buzz that lasts all night. And in Chinese tea gardens, tea-drinkers prefer to drink their beverage at room temperature and, according to European tourists, strain the tea leaves through their teeth. Just remember, however people take their tea, they all start with boiling water.

HOW TO SHAKE HANDS

❖

Handshakes differ in force, frequency, and occasion from culture to culture. In France, office colleagues start the day by shaking hands and old friends meeting for dinner begin and end the evening with handshakes all around. In West African countries, rather than refuse you his dirty right hand, a farmer will extend his right wrist for you to shake. And in cultures where the handshake is an exotic import, you may find yourself holding a hand so inanimate as to put you in mind of a department store mannequin or a corpse.

It's said that in the beginning the purpose of a hand-shake was to demonstrate two parties' good intentions by showing that both came to the meeting empty-handed (i.e., neither one was concealing a weapon). One palm to another was the quintessential contract; beyond words or meaningful looks, a handshake sealed the deal. Nowadays lawyers and metal detectors serve that purpose and a handshake is the friendly way to acknowledge another person's presence, especially a person to whom one is being introduced or hasn't seen in a while. The hand-shake is more formal than a nod of the head, less familiar than a peck on the cheek. Properly executed, it's an excellent way of engaging the social gears.

In American culture, a good, firm handshake is admired. How does one achieve that ideal? The best way is to take a firm, but not bone-crushing, grip on the whole hand of the person you're being introduced to— more on that later—and shake it up and down. Avoid a back and forth motion. More than three times up and down and it will look as if you're recreating a Three Stooges routine. Nor, unless you're a minister or a grand-mother, should you retain the hand you're shaking. In most circumstances, a grip and a modified pump does the job.

Why do we specify "the whole hand"? Because two fingers just won't do. Neither will the tips of your fingers. The palm of your hand should rest in the palm of the other person's hand. The bases of your thumbs should lock. Suit the firmness of your grip to that of the person whose hand you're taking. If it's a child who's just learning the procedure, go easy. If it's a person much older than yourself, what seems like a normal handshake to you might be uncomfortable to them, old bones being subject to aches and pains unknown to youth. And it may happen that you're being introduced to a person whose right hand is somehow out of commission—in a sling or bandaged or disabled. If the left hand is extended, take it. He or she has been in this situation many more times than you, so follow his or her lead.

"A handshake like a dead fish" is not the worst thing that can be attributed to a person but it's not exactly a compliment. (Logically, the opposite, having a handshake like a live fish, should constitute a compliment of the first order but the expression doesn't seem to have caught on.) Think of your own reaction when a lifeless hand is placed in yours. You want to drop it immediately and wipe your fingers on the nearest towel. Or the draperies. Moreover, in addition to the immediate physical reaction, such handshakes give rise to all kinds of unwarranted speculation about the bad handshaker's character and upbringing. Genuine as these reactions may be, they're a bit extreme. A firm handshake will spare you and others such unpleasantness.

The appropriately firm handshake is accompanied by a warm smile. Also and always, look the person whose hand you are shaking in the eye. It's the American way. In other cultures, lowered eyes bespeak humility or modesty. Here, people will just think you're shifty.

If you live in a cold climate, don't forget to remove your glove or mitten when shaking hands. Unless, of course, frozen sleet is raining from the heavens or your arms are full of groceries. The other point of the extended open hand, beyond showing that you're not carrying a dagger, is, literally, to press the flesh, to make physical contact with the person you're greeting. Although not as displeasing as the limp handshake and the averted gaze, a gloved one only half accomplishes its purpose.

Often, a handshake takes place when you're being introduced to someone for the first time. So, just so you know what's proper, we'll take a paragraph or two to tell you about introductions and who gets presented to whom and in what order. Some introductions are so informal and include so many people at once, that a nod and a smile do duty for the handshake. Suppose you come into a party where people are already standing around talking to one another. Everyone is pretty much the same age. The person doing the introducing brings you up to the first conversational group and says, "Janet, this is Richard, Susan, Sally, uh, Jennifer, Jason, and Jennifer's sister, Lee. Guys, this is Janet." Everyone then says, "Hi," and you, Janet, are supposed to consider yourself introduced.

If only two people are being introduced in similarly informal circumstances, introductions proceed according to status (i.e., you introduce the person you know less well to the person you know better). "Jim, this is Richard Dorment. We went to college together. Richard,

Jim Page." Whereupon Richard and Jim shake hands.

When the people to be introduced are of different ages and sexes, there's an order to follow. The order is based on an endangered convention: Age is deserving of greater deference than youth and women of greater deference than men. Therefore, you introduce the younger person to the older and the man to the woman. The younger man gets introduced to the older, "Uncle Arthur, I'd like to introduce my next-door neighbor, Steven Moore." A man is introduced to a woman who's more or less the same age as he is, "Lola, I want you to meet my brother, Jim Pinfold" or "Mother, this is Sam St. Pierre, the gentleman from whom we're renting the boat." And, since age takes precedence over sex, you introduce the younger woman to the older man, "Dad, this is my writing partner, Edith Hazard" or "Mr. St. Pierre, I don't think you've met my sister, Fran Phillips." Then, both parties extend their right hands, shake, and say something like, "How do you do?" or "Hello, how nice to meet you." In an earlier generation, the man waited for the woman to extend her hand before offering his own. Nowadays, it doesn't matter who makes the first move. Similarly, it used to be that a woman could remain seated while introductions were being made (unless they were being made to an older woman) but a man was always expected to stand up. For youth to sit while age stands, especially when introductions are being made, is still bad form.

Sometimes introductions don't take. There was a lot of noise. There were too many people. Or time has had its way with memory. It's not uncommon to run across someone to whom you've already been introduced, perhaps more than once, and not come up with a name. If you pass on the street or in the corridor, a smile and a nod are perfectly adequate. Nothing obliges you to admit the face looks familiar but you haven't a clue as to why. If, however, you find yourself together in a meeting or at a party and you still can't come up with a name and the look on that familiar face signals an equivalent lapse of memory, the easy thing to do is extend your hand, announce your name, and hope they'll do the same. If, surprisingly, Mr. X. says, "Hello, Otto," and doesn't follow through with his own name; or merely perversely replies, "Yes, I remember," then too bad for you and low marks for him. You're playing the game and he's either trying to score points or is too dim to have understood why you might be reintroducing yourself.

HOW TO GIVE DIRECTIONS

❖

Giving accurate, surefire, easy-to-follow directions is as simple as living by the Golden Rule. Do unto others as you would have others do unto you. Put yourself in the other guy's shoes—or behind that person's steering wheel—and imagine the kind of directions you would like to receive. Not too wordy. Not too many false starts based on unfamiliar local references. Just enough prominent landmarks, route numbers, or street names to get you where you want to go. Approximate distances are a help too, if they're not excessively approximate.

If you're not a hermit, you'll find yourself explaining how to get to where you live over and over again. This is a first-rate opportunity for you to improve your ability to give directions. When somebody asks you, it won't be as if you've never been asked the question before. Nor should it take you by surprise. Indeed, considering the number of times you've successfully arrived at your own address, you're something of an expert. You can turn this expertise to your friends' advantage by giving flawless instructions. If they never show up, you'll know the directions aren't flawless. You've left out something crucial. You'll also know because the errant friends will tell you. Chances are that you can count on a frank, even brutal, appraisal of your skills in this department. Don't despair. This will allow you to rectify the error next time out. Practice makes perfect. Before long your directions will be so accurate that everyone you want to arrive at your front door will be able to do so.

The degree of detail you include depends on two things: The familiarity of the people you're directing with the general area and, harder to calculate, their ability to follow the directions you give them. Some people, when in doubt or confused, simply swing their car, bicycle, or moped off the main thoroughfare at their very first opportunity to turn right—exit ramp, dirt road, cow path, it makes no difference. It's a conditioned reflex. Like cats that come running when they hear the clink of a can opener on metal. Or perhaps it's a genetic predisposition, like sneezing when moving from artificial lighting into sunlight. Reverse conditioning is not your responsibility. Neither is fooling with people's DNA. There's not a thing you can do about people who will get lost. Just be prepared to hold dinner.

If you like, you can measure out the mile and two-eighths they're supposed to drive after they pass the cemetery on the left. But unless you're living someplace on the Great Plains where one telephone pole looks much like another or in the North Woods where the same goes for the murmuring pines and the hemlocks, exact mileage may not be as useful as landmarks. We're not talking about landmarks like, "You know where the old Rialto used to be, well, it's a parking lot now, you go past that . . ." Such directions are useful if the person to whom you're giving the instructions spent her girlhood in the town; if not, no use at all. Similarly useless is the wandering reminiscence, "So you turn left at the second stoplight, right there where they have those beautiful magnolias every spring. Of course this spring it was so cold it was practically April before they blossomed and after old man Moody painted his house pink you could hardly see them anyway." All this will be pretty fascinating when you're taking your friends on a walking tour of the neighborhood, but the point now is to spare them an unplanned tour of the same. Save the local color and the home-improvements anecdote for later.

If you're giving instructions to a stranger, you already know she doesn't know the area or she wouldn't be asking how to get to Orr's Island in the first place. But can she follow the directions you're about to give her? (We'll say it's "her" because men seem to prefer to circle a city for hours, or traverse several counties before stopping to ask. Not so with more practical-minded women.)

Concentrate on giving clear-cut, one-of-a-kind directions: "You cross the bridge and drive halfway up the hill to the stoplight. You'll pass a Getty station on your right. Turn right at the light and then take your second left. That'll be Perkins Street. We're the first house on the left."

Stoplights, railroad tracks, bridges, and conspicuous, one-of-a-kind buildings are the currency of reliable

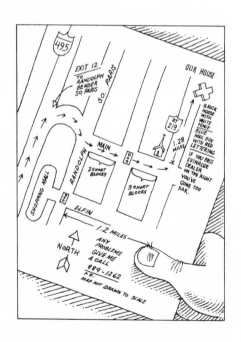

directions. A little built-in redundancy—street names in addition to landmarks and stoplights, distances in miles if the interval between landmarks is important—may help. So will fail-safe warnings like, "If you come to the water tower, you've gone too far," or, "If the pavement ends, you missed our mailbox; it's the next-to-last one before the dirt road begins."

Obviously, if you're writing down directions to send to everyone invited to the seventy-fifth birthday celebration, you can go on at greater length than you would if you're giving them out over the telephone or in person. Writing them down forces you to edit a bit and spares your friends the stream-of-consciousness style that seems so natural in an oral presentation. In written as in oral directions, your goal is the same—to provide the necessary minimum of information.

If asked for directions to a place you don't know how to get to, say so. Spare the lost tourist your apologies and your good intentions. Spare yourself their unheard curses when you've sent them in exactly the wrong direction. Say you don't know and let them ask someone who might.

If you know vaguely where an address is—it's on the eastern side of town but you're in the west—give the inquirer information to get him or her to the neighborhood in question and tell them to ask when they get there.

Avoid concluding your directions with the phrase, "You can't miss it." It may be true, it may be false, but it tends to provoke uneasy laughter and shake the confidence of the very people you're hoping to reassure.

Coda: **How to Read a Map**

Standard road maps invariably contain more information than you require to find your way. Put another way, more complimentary to the cartographer, you can ignore some of the facts a well-made road map contains if all you want to do is get yourself from point A to point B. You don't need to know to the nearest 10,000 how many people live in the towns and cities en route. Nor when same towns and cities were incorporated. You'll be a better person for knowing that Concord is the state capital of New Hampshire, that the northern part of the state is dotted with ski resorts and that there are even some airports here and there. But these stray facts will not help you in your mission.

What you do need to know is, "Are we going in the right direction?" The question has resonance at many levels. What is man's fate? Are we truly happy with the course of the American republic these last ten years? More specifically, are we really headed west? The question can be couched in metaphysical terms: What is the relation between reality—you at the wheel of a moving car—and the map you've unwadded from the glove compartment? Take your choice. You can work from the map to reality or from reality to the map. In either case, it helps to know which way north is. On a map, it's the top of the sheet. In a car, it all depends. The sun may help you. If the sun is shining directly into your eyes and it's around 5:00 P.M., there's a good chance you're headed toward the Pacific Ocean. If you're not inclined to trust the evidence of your senses and prefer a technological fix, a dashboard compass could be the answer. And it doesn't hurt to remember that odd-numbered interstates run north and south, even-numbered, east and west, and interstates with numbers like 295, 495, and 695 are liable to be ringroads or beltways, running around metropolitan areas.

It's also useful to you to make a connection between the road you're on and the lines and numbers on the map. What's the number of the road you're on? Can you or your navigator find it on the map? Good. Is it headed in the direction you want to go? No? Not nearly? Better pull over and get your bearings.

How to do that? It's useful to know, for example, what kind of road you're on at present. County road? Interstate? (If it's the latter, take heart; you may be nowhere near where you want to be going but you can't be very lost either.) And how is the kind of road you're on depicted on the unwadded map you've spread out over the steering wheel? While you're trying to figure out where you are, note the difference between how a divided highway and a two-way undivided highway shows up on the map, the difference between paved and unpaved, between U.S. Interstate, U.S. Federal, and State roads. (These differences will be indicated not only by the color and width of the line representing the roads on the map, but also by the color and style of the figures designating route number. The shields in which the route number is contained on the map may or may not match up with the signage observed along the road.) You know, for example, that you turned off the interstate at Exit 28 but that was fifteen minutes ago and now you're on a gravel road. Can you find that on the map? Not if you don't know how gravel roads are represented. There it is and there's the mistake. You followed your friends' advice and took the first right after the railroad tracks but clearly the road to Stickney Corners is the county road just beyond. Now you have reality in synch with its Platonic ideal (the map) and can proceed.

HOW TO APPLY
EIGHTH GRADE MATH

❖

Before the advent of the drug era and all its attendant distrust, a glazed expression on the face of an otherwise bright-eyed thirteen-year-old was routinely attributed to the child's fear of higher mathematics. Or even not-so-high mathematics. The proliferation of hand calculators and the presence of computers in every classroom has thinned the ranks of those self-described as being "hopeless with numbers." But if they're no longer terrified, it's only because terror has been contained by "electronic-tutor" dependency. They're handicapped, but they can function. Still and all, the chronically phobic, those who are truly gaga when someone mentions "tip," "circumference," or "lira"—that group is still alive. And what is being done for these poor souls? Very little. Misdiagnosed and misunderstood, the innumerate will live on, avoiding numbers at all costs, seeking the companionship of those who can count higher than ten without removing their socks and are therefore at ease in all social situations where mathematical calculations may be required. Whether that relationship simply enables the mathophobe to become increasingly incapable of basic math or it begins to reveal a host of other defective personality traits (tardiness, untidiness) is a question for another book.

Banking

Cars that sport the I MUST HAVE MONEY, I STILL HAVE CHECKS bumper sticker are driven by mathophobes. Everyone knows someone who admits that he never balances his checkbook. Raised eyebrows notwithstanding, this irresponsible fellow and his many brothers and sisters are allowed to open checking accounts along with the rest of the world. Banks try to accommodate them by sending statements out on a monthly basis. If your bank has a cash machine, you can find out how much is left in your account anonymously—avoiding the teller's eye-rolling, audible sighing, pencil-tapping impatience . . . it's the third time this week!

But what if your curiosity is not merely academic? What if you aren't at the bank, what if you are in the department store and you want to buy the last navy blue Ralph Lauren blazer on the rack, at an unbelievably reduced price, that six people just your size are waiting to try on?

Learning to keep a running balance in your checkbook is like learning to brush your teeth. The action itself is not difficult to master; it's keeping at it that counts. It's really not the math—you can use a calculator if you think you'll make a mistake in subtraction—it's the habit. Once you've acquired it, you won't feel quite right if you haven't done it. A two-step process may help: First, write out the stub *before* you write out the check. That way you'll be able to work with some reliable records and have no need of hypnosis or past-life regression to figure out what happened to checks 901, 902, and 910 through 913. Second, establish a routine whereby you balance the book once a week at the same time you do some other weekly chore. Tie it to vacuuming, the laundry, riding to work on Monday morning. Or associate it with a weekly event like before you sit down to watch "Monday Night Football" or listen to the Metropolitan Opera on Saturday afternoon. If you balance the book weekly and square it with the bank statement monthly, you'll no longer be in a financial fog.

Tipping

"What percentage do you use?" you ask your luncheon companions, stalling for time and preferring to appear dim or cheap, preferring death by dismemberment to calculating the 15 or 20 percent it's your responsibility to leave. The table has been cleared, you have thanked the host profusely and insisted on leaving the tip, people have put their coats on and you buy a little more time by saying you'll have to get change from the cashier.

A minimum of mental arithmetic will spare you, your friends, and the service staff of the restaurant this charade. If the service was better than average and your host is a regular patron, the tip is 20 percent of the bill, either with or without the tax, whichever is going to make the calculation easier. Let's say the bill for coffee and pie for the five of you came to $16.86. Round it off to $17.00. Take 10 percent of $17.00—or move the decimal point one space to the left—and double it: 10 percent of $17.00 = $1.70 × 2 = $3.40. Leave $3.50. Simple, no?

Ah, but what if we get into higher figures? The very same principles apply. On a bill of $45.78, round it to the next higher figure, $46.00. Take 10 percent and multiply it by 2. You get $9.20. If your calculation included the tax, you can round down, leaving a tip of $9.00. If you excluded the tax, better round up to $9.50 or $10.00. You can do the calculation on your fingers under the table if necessary. Just try not to move your lips. (Regardless of your mathematical prowess, note: 15 percent is acceptable in a slumping economy, 20 is generous and appreciated, and 10 percent is barely thanks, even if the math is easier.)

Math rules

Who could wait to graduate from eighth grade math? Never again would we have to figure out the circumference of a circle, or the perimeter of a rectangle. Who cares about square feet, fulcrums, and arcs? One more week and school is out. But when, twenty years later, some kid at the truck rental place wants to know, "What size truck do you want? You know, like, how many cubic feet you gonna need to haul all your stuff?" Mrs. McDermott's wagging finger wags again, and you are as tongue-tied today as you used to be at the blackboard. You've forgotten the formula for cubic feet . . . come to think of it, you never actually knew it. And now who are you going to ask . . . the babysitter . . . the waiter? . . . a long distance call to Mrs. McDermott? Naaah. It's time to review.

The formula for cubic feet is simple: Multiply height times length times width. So if you need to transport a refrigerator (approx. $6' \times 3' \times 3' = 54$ cubic feet), a sofa (approx. $8' \times 2.5' \times 3.5' = 70$ cubic feet), and six chairs ($4' \times 2.5' \times 2.5' = 25 \times 6$ of them $= 150$ cubic feet), you would need a truck or trailer that could hold 274 cubic feet, plus a little room for maneuvering things around, and a dolly because you aren't strong enough to get everything on the truck by yourself.

The formula for square feet is even simpler: Multiply height times length. You have decided to paint your living room spruce green. You walk into the hardware store and pick up a gallon of paint and read the label. It says the contents of the can will cover 400 square feet. Will one can be enough, the helpful clerk queries? Good question. At this point you can throw yourself on the mercy of the merchant (who gets a bonus for the most paint sold at the end of the month) or make the modest purchase of a tape measure and go back to the apartment for some quick measurements. Back at the apartment you find that two of the boring Navajo white walls measure 14' by 8.25', which equals 115.5 square feet—there are two of them, so that's 231'. The third wall is 10' by 8.25' (that's easy, right?) so you have to add in another 82.5' to the 231' (313.5') and the fourth wall, opening to the hall, is 5' by 8.25' (41.25') and you race back to the hardware store clerk and shout "356.75 square feet!" Proud hardly covers it. One gallon probably will. Note: If you have three windows and two doors in this room, you need to recalculate because they will either be a different color or will require a different kind of paint. You figure the area of the windows and doors using the same formula and subtract the total from your original total. Easy as pie. (That's P-I-E.)

Speaking of pi (π), we honestly couldn't think of a reason to use the formula for the size of a circle. Perhaps if you are about to harvest a circular cornfield . . . or, you wanted to make a Christmas tree skirt for your mother-in-law . . . who knows why, but you might need it. Following the spirit of math rules, here it is: For the circumference of a circle (that's the outside measurement of the circle) you multiply $2 \times \pi \times R$ or 2 times 3.14 times the radius (the length of a straight line from the center of the circle to the circumference). For the area of the circle you multiply π (3.14) times the R (radius), squared. Imagine you have nothing to do one afternoon and you are particularly hungry. You look over the Pizza Parlor menu and try to decide whether it would be cheaper to order four small pizzas or two large ones. The small pizzas are 8" (radius is 4") for $5.00, the large pizzas are 12" (radius 6") for $10.00. For $20.00 worth of small pizza you will get ($3.14 \times 16 = 50.24$ sq. inches $\times 4 = 200.96$ sq. in.) 201 square inches of pizza; for $20.00 worth of large pizza you will get ($3.14 \times 36 = 113.04$ sq. inches $\times 2 = 226.08$ sq. in.) or 226 square inches of pizza. If you've stayed with this, the money saver is the two-large-pizzas order. If you haven't, you probably decided to go with a meatball sandwich for $8.50 twenty minutes ago.

Exchange bureau

Travel abroad is an enriching experience. The art, the history, the music, the food, the foreignness of it all—indeed every single thing is wonderful until it is time to pay. Not necessarily because you are low on funds, but rather because it takes a tremendous effort to figure out the actual cost . . . "You know, I mean in dollars, how much is it?" For the truly innumerate, there is the play money approach. It's a little risky, but it's been known to work. Ignore the exchange rate. Stop thinking in terms of dollars, just think in terms of trade. It's a lot like playing Monopoly, and sometimes the paper currency looks as if you are. At the beginning of the trip, convert one half of the traveling money into the currency of choice. Divide the number of days in your vacation by half, and divide that figure into the amount of currency you received at the exchange bureau. The answer is roughly what you have to spend per day for the first half of your vacation. Before it is time to go for dinner, shop around, compare prices on the menus posted outside the restaurants, get an idea for what would be reasonable, and then go in and enjoy your meal. When the check arrives (what a break, the tip's included), be sure you are using the correct denominations—10,000 looks so much like 100,000, and sometimes the bigger coins are worth less than the medium-sized ones.

Of course, the real way to do this exchange rate business is to know the ratio of dollars to the currency of choice. Hypothetically, for the sake of the exercise, say to yourself, one dollar is worth X number of marks (or francs, drachma, or cedi). Now, translate the same idea into the language of eighth grade math: the *ratio* of dollars to marks is 1 to X. So, if you are desperate to know "how much you've *really* spent" and "*really*" means "if you were back home," you simply divide the amount of the dinner check by the exchange rate, et voilà, you will have the satisfaction of knowing the dollar value of your meal. Of course, satisfaction comes to all of us in different forms, and for those who have read this chapter surreptitiously, it most probably arrived with the first taste of veal piccata . . . well before the check is presented.

HOW TO SET
A MOUSETRAP

❖

Peripheral vision must be next to extra sensory perception on the great line of sensory experiences, either that or at the opposite end of the spectrum—like politicians who are identified as being either so far to the left or the right that they actually agree on one or two issues. On some "Believe It or Not" TV shows, and always in the tabloids sold near the grocery's checkout counter, instances of ESP are reported. The man who walks into his shop and clearly sees a Martian leaving by the back door; the housewife who swears she passed a perfect stranger on the stairs—later identified as her husband's very late great-great-great-grandfather. Both mention the feeling of a definite presence. At the other end of the spectrum, we remember grade school, when height was of minimal concern, and kids were told by their basketball coach that increasing one's peripheral vision is key to the game. But what exactly was it? Well, it turned out to be something like having eyes in the back of your head (the math teacher and your mother had them, why shouldn't you?), and according to the coach, it was a skill, something you could work on. In a way, peripheral vision is close to ESP, closer still to somehow being there ahead of time.

The positive side of having a mouse in your house is that its presence gives you an opportunity to experience the exact point at which sensing and seeing meet. For a few days you are troubled by the sense that you are not alone in the apartment. You're not superstitious and there are no ghosts in the family's history, but there is an unmistakable presence, fleeting, but a presence nevertheless, and you wonder if you don't need a vacation or at least a rest. Ignore the presence, and other signs will appear to vouch for it. Cracker boxes once full will have been emptied, quite neatly, from the bottom. Oversized jimmies (you don't have chocolate sprinkles in your pantry?) are found on your kitchen counter. During cocktails, you glance toward the kitchen and see—my God, it *is* a mouse—helping itself to the dessert cheese. You move quickly to close the door on the scene but not quickly enough to stop the culprit from leaping to the floor, racing through the doorway you were hoping to seal, over your sandaled foot, and making a clean escape along the backside of the couch where three unsuspecting dinner guests are holding forth on the "moments in history" from The New Hampshire Primary. The conversation is uninterrupted, you take a deep (inaudible) breath, and thank God not one of the guests played basketball in grade school.

The guests have gone home. It was a lovely evening. And you are momentarily relieved to know that you haven't been dreaming, there really was someone in the apartment with you all this time. Now the question is what to do about it. You know mice are a nuisance, and you can't afford to keep them around. Not only will they continue to eat your food, and often your library, but they multiply like crazy. In fact, the first mouse you catch should be buried with a vow to catch its mate (they never seem to travel alone).

In the morning you set out for the hardware store/grocery store/feed store (depending on where you live), practicing the embarrassing line, "Do you sell mousetraps?" It's sort of like asking the pharmacist for a shampoo that will take care of head lice. No matter how often the exterminator or the school nurse tells you, "This happens to the nicest people," it always feels uncomfortably connected to an inattention to cleanliness. Well, it does happen to nice people, and to not-so-nice people, and you just have to walk in and act as if your question is as normal as one about laundry detergent. You may be surprised to learn that there are different size traps available. The bigger one is for rats. Take one look, and be glad your problems can be solved with the economy size.

So, for $2.98 you've purchased this slip of wood with its metal spring, and brought it home in a brown paper bag. What seemed to be your mouse's favorite food? Tom and Jerry always used the cheese-as-bait method, but if you don't have cheese in the house, a cracker or Cheerios (stick them on with peanut butter), a raisin, or even a scrap of lettuce will work. Also think about where you have most often felt you were in the presence of this furry little nuisance. On the counter in the kitchen? Along the mop board, on top of the icebox, in the pantry? Wherever it is, you should consider setting the trap and leaving it there (*remembering* that it is there so that you don't inadvertently trap your middle toe the next morning). It can take several days before you have any results. The creature may be something of a magician, able to lift your bait without triggering the spring, which in turn makes you believe that the trap doesn't work . . . whap goes the bar, crushing your thumb, jump-starting your heart. You have disregarded the warning on the trap—the one about touching the mechanism once it has been set—and as you hop and howl around the apartment, shaking your hand and cursing the manufacturer, be certain that the mouse is reeling with laughter in the next room. So some mice are more clever than others. Set the trap again, but try to *attach* the bait to the platform (again, peanut butter helps). If three or four days have gone by, and you are only feeding this foe rather than entrapping it, you might consider putting out two or three traps. Again, do what you can to remember exact locations. Weekend guests are invariably put off by an unexpected SNAP!

How to set the trap
Generally speaking, a mousetrap has four pieces: the base, most often made of wood; a metal arm loosely attached at one end of the base; a spring-loaded metal piece mounted at the middle of the base (outlining the perimeter of the base, this apparatus is unlike the guillotine—effectiveness depends solely upon the force of the blow); and a plate attached just beyond the spring with room for an irresistible piece of cheese and a small opening for the end of the arm. Stick the cheese, peanut butter, or raisin to this plate. Then, holding the trap by the sides (keeping your fingers clear of the spring), pull the spring all the way back and hold it firmly against the base. Swing the arm over the spring. Stop shaking, continue holding the spring, and tip the base toward you so that the baited plate lifts up. Carefully hook the end of

the arm into the opening at the bottom of the plate. The arm, its tip wedged into the opening of the plate, now restrains the spring-loaded bait. The trap is set, and all you have to do is put it down in the appropriate place without releasing it. Not as easy as it sounds, and guaranteed to make you jump if you goof. Private practice sessions are encouranged; the startle is worth a million laughs, but you may tire of hearing the story. Private or public, the practice is important for a second reason: The Dilemma of Success. Unloading a mousetrap is not a pleasant chore for anyone, but if you were fumbling with a chunk of cheese, image how you'll do with a cold carcass. If you haven't had time to practice, or you just can't bring yourself to think of touching the thing ("What if it's not dead; what if it's only sleeping?") you should plan to absorb the cost of the trap. Then, open a grocery bag, place the opening next to the trap, avert your eyes, hum a tune, sweep the trapped mouse into the bag, close securely and toss into the nearest dumpster.

A word about other methods. Hoping the problem will go away is not an option. Living in denial serves only to swell the enemy's ranks. There is the old tried-and-true rodent poison. Some people swear by it. There are detailed instructions on the box (found in grocery stores across the land), but in those instructions no mention is made of at least two reasons why this is not always the best solution. The first has to do with where the mouse is living. If the two of you are in an older building, one with walls made from lath and plaster and plenty of openings—no radon fears for you—the wall may be honeycombed with an elaborate system of roadways accessible only to mice. A mouse that has been poisoned can choose its burial site, and if it turns out to be "along old Highway 65," you will have the benefit of a terrible (unmistakable) odor for at least two weeks after the wake, and all you can do is apologize for it. The other problem has to do with the possibility that your mouse's dying wish is to become an actor. Wish granted, the poisoned mouse wobbles out from hiding onto the center of your living-room carpet and, without paying the slightest attention to the shooing or screaming of your guests, presents a unique intrepretation of scenes from *La Bohème* and *Swan Lake*. It is a performance not to be believed, nor will it ever be forgotten, so why chance it? Everyone agrees that an alert mouse will be less embarrassing in the long run, and that a sudden death is the preferred short run.

If you are extremely tenderhearted or a principled vegetarian ("It has nothing to do with cholesterol, I just can't bear the thought of killing"), impractical Have-a-

Heart traps are available at the hardware store. The idea is that you trap the mouse, but you don't hurt it. Then you release it, still unhurt, so it can pursue other career options. Before you take this nonviolent approach, ask yourself if it makes any sense. Can you picture riding the Seventh Avenue bus, the loaded trap on your lap concealed by your favorite Hungarian shawl, hoping that no one will be at your stop, that no one will watch as you attach a long string to the trap door, that no one will wonder why you are standing on the park bench repeatedly jerking a small cage up off the sidewalk and slamming it back down again?

What if you have just moved into a house that has been empty for some time with the unfortunately obvious exception of four-legged creatures? Traps by the hundreds is not the answer. A bigger, four-legged feline-type creature may be. Mice tend to pack up in the middle of the night when a cat moves in. Of course, if cats aren't your thing or you just aren't quite ready for the responsibility or your landlord has tied the security deposit to the no-pet clause, you can ask at the office if anyone wants to send his or her cat on a weekend safari . . . all you can eat. No takers? Call your landlord and offer to line up an exterminator, "Shall I have them send the bill to your home address or to the office?" Then, make plans to take a long weekend.

This is not the time to reread *Stuart Little* or to rent the *Cinderella* video. Procrastination will lead to christening the little critters. Thinking of your tormentors as small furry humanoids will be followed by unbearable guilt, which in turn only validates procrastination. This vicious cycle will eventually turn you into a Screaming Minnie—sorry, that's Meemie—who spends lunch hours in the library alternately looking through today's rental listings and tracing the Pied Piper's ancestral chart.

HOW TO
LAY A FIRE

❖

Picture the perfect living room. Comfortable furniture, walls lined with books, and a magnificent fireplace. What more could anyone ask? Well, you could ask if the fireplace works. But if you do, you should be prepared for, "We don't know, we've never used it." Or, "Oh, do you know something about fireplaces?" Followed by, "I would so love to have a fire, it would *make* the party." At which point you can either politely agree in an apologetic tone (which should clearly take you off the detail) or ask to be pointed in the direction of the woodpile. Ninety-three percent of the guests will favor the first response, as well they should. After all, those same people probably have little experience with fires and fireplaces, be they in mansions or ski lodges—and what hostess plans an evening well enough to include the comings and goings of a charging fire brigade? However, if you are in the top 7 percent, reserved for outing club members and a scout or two, you will no doubt welcome the opportunity to be an obliging guest. And if you would like to move into that select group, these instructions may be followed as part of your initiation.

Probably the most important step is to determine if you have a "working" chimney. During the *daytime* the easiest way to do this is with a small mirror. Unfortunately the likelihood of someone carrying a compact is not as good as it used to be, but try to be resourceful. There may be some tinfoil in the kitchen, or a shiny top of a pot, the blade of a Swiss army knife or, if you are lucky, the bottom of a glass may do the trick. You need something that will allow you to look up the chimney (without having to put your head inside the chimney), and you are hoping that that something will refract light from the top letting you know that there is a clear passage from the bottom up. You may see no light at all because of the damper (an obstructing metal plate inside the chimney), a chimney cap, or a squirrel's nest. Can you find the handle for the damper? In older fireplaces a metal handle is often found inside the chimney (a good reason to find it before you light the fire). The handle could also be at the end of a long chain inside the chimney. Just give it a tug. If you can't locate the handle, try reaching up the chimney and pushing the front or the back of the damper up. Success will be accompanied by an audible "clunk." Try your mirror again. It should give you an indication that the smoke will find its way directly up and into the atmosphere.

If you still have no reading of light, go outside and check for a chimney cap or, more likely, some evidence of a squirrel's nest sticking out of the top. Getting onto the roof and removing the cap or nest should be considered worthwhile only if there is no other source of heat in the house and/or no other place to spend your weekend. That being the case, you have bitten off more than the average person wishes to chew and at the same time you probably have a pretty good idea of how to get up onto the roof, so words of caution and care will be wasted. One note: Should you open the damper and then find that the chimney is still closed off, be sure to close the damper. It helps to discourage little furry animals from making their way down into the house, where the havoc they will wreak is not to be believed.

If it is nighttime and you can open the damper but still are not sure about the chimney, light the corner of a *small* piece of paper. If the smoke goes straight up, you are probably okay. To be doubly sure, try lighting a larger piece of paper and see what happens. "Why not use this 'check' daytime or nighttime?" one might ask. The smoke from one piece of paper may rest inside a sealed chimney, waiting for the smoke from a well-laid fire to force it down into the room. The theory is that a little puff is better than a cloud, but no puff at all is best.

Once you have every indication that the chimney is clear, it is time to lay the fire. You will need: Dry wood, kindling (scraps of wood, dry branches, heavy cardboard), paper, and matches. If you cannot find dry wood or kindling, but there is wet or rotten wood, try making Cape Cod kindling. Take two sheets of newspaper and make a tight roll, starting with the bottom right corner and rolling up to the top left corner. Holding the ends of the roll, tie it into a double knot. The result is a tight wad of paper that takes longer to burn. No newspaper to be found? Do what you can with paper products . . . toilet paper isn't particularly flammable, but its cardboard tube is. As a last resort, look for some Alaskan kindling (known in most places as kerosene—NOT TO BE CONFUSED WITH GASOLINE. If you are not sure which is which, DON'T go any farther—you could blow up the house). Take the wood outside and soak two logs with ½ cup of kerosene, enough to get a flame going that will eventually dry out the wood and then burn it. The rest of the wet wood should be placed near the fire so that it will dry out in time to keep the fire going.

Split wood burns more quickly than wood that has simply been cut. If there is some sort of woodshed on the property or a collection of tools in one of the closets, you may be able to find a splitting maul or axe (the maul is the weapon of choice, it's bigger, heavier, and not so sharp). An axe will do, but it requires more strength and often gets caught in the grain.

The art of splitting wood is enhanced by an appreciation of basic physics. The act of splitting wood is awesome. Once again, practice makes perfect. So if there are plenty of unsplit logs around, and you want to work on that frontier image while building up a welcome pile of split pieces and a sweat that temporarily eliminates the need for the fire you were working on, go to it. Stand the log up on its end on a stump or larger log, using the handle of the maul to measure the exact distance between it and your body. The idea is that the weight of the maul, plus the force of the swing, will do the splitting for you. Spread your feet apart (and for heaven's sakes don't do this in Birkenstocks), blow into your cupped hands to warm them (cold hands slip easily on cold wooden handles), grab onto the handle with your favored hand ten inches from the base, place the other hand just below. Ever play baseball? Really?

Measure the distance one more time to be sure you are on target, then put the maul over your head (your elbows will be just behind your ears), and bring it forward, up, over, and down all in one fluid motion. Nice work!

On to the laying of the fire. Remember eighth grade science? Fire requires a constant supply of oxygen, so airflow is key. Clean out the ashes that are in the fireplace, enough so that air can circulate underneath the logs as they rest on the grate or andirons. No grate? No andirons? Or did you say, "I don't know what an andiron is?" They are iron supports to hold logs in the fireplace, according to the dictionary. If there are none, look outside for some large rocks or bricks to work as substitutes. Place two logs on the andirons, stuffing loose wads of newspaper (three sheets is usually ample) between them. Allowing for some space between the back of the fireplace and the first log, try to place the fire well inside the mouth of the chimney (i.e., not out in the room). Two logs sandwiching three wads of newspaper form the first layer (fig. 1). For the second layer, place kindling on

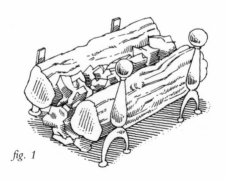

fig. 1

fig. 2

top of paper and logs in a diagonal pattern, leaving enough space (perhaps an inch) between pieces for easy airflow (fig. 2). A third log is placed at an angle on top of the kindling, so that from above the three logs roughly form the letter N or Z (fig. 3).

Most chimneys are stubborn when cold. To keep the smoke inside the room to a minimum, try holding a

fig. 3

piece of newspaper up inside the chimney and lighting it. You may need to do this three or four times before the chimney is warm enough to draw the smoke from your fire. When you see that the smoke from the newspaper is going up quite readily, it is time to light the fire. Sit back, relax, and enjoy the warmth of the blaze.

Cautionary note: While it may be tempting to burn empty cereal boxes, Christmas wrapping paper, paper plates from the party, etc., you shouldn't. Excess paper tends to rush partway up the chimney before it is completely burned, which, in turn, can cause a chimney fire or a fire on your roof.

Fire is as dangerous as it is effective. Be careful. If there is an extinguisher (one that was inspected recently) keep it handy. If there isn't, think about what you would use to put out a fire (a bucket of sand, water, snow). Run over the possibilities before you light the fire. Put a screen in front of the fire if you plan to leave the room. No screen? Do what you can to push the burning logs to the back of the fireplace. At that picturesque mountain cabin, "Close the Damper" should be on your final departure checklist. (You do have a checklist, don't you?)

HOW TO BE A
WONDERFUL WEEKEND GUEST

❖

Riffling through the usual bills and the third-class trash that your postman delivers, you stop midshuffle in disbelief. There, between the note from MasterCard and a clever plea from your local PBS station, is an envelope—a hand-addressed envelope. Even if you were expecting what appears to be a personal invitation, its actual arrival is worth ten seconds of excitement at the very least. We'll assume that this invitation is not from your stodgy Great Aunt Harriet who continually crusades against the genetic gaucherie credited to your mother's side of the family. No, you are being invited to visit friends at their house for a weekend. The prospects are very bright, indeed. You already know that you enjoy their company, your calendar is clear, and you have enough time and money to get there and back. So, pick up your pen, as they have done, and let them know that you are delighted to accept their kind invitation and supply specific information about your plans for arrival and departure. Signed and sealed, the acceptance is on its way, and you begin to imagine dinner table conversations in which everyone finds you witty and charming beyond belief and walks along country lanes in which your dazzling repertoire of bird calls is universally admired.

Some claim that anticipation is nine-tenths of the experience. Preparation is the other tenth. And before you leave, before you even start the laundry or dig out the duffel bag, your preparation should begin with a brief study in comparative finances:

Are your hosts: (a) worth millions?
(b) making about what you are making?
(c) trying to send five of their six kids through college on unemployment benefits?

And are you: (a) worth millions?
(b) in their comfort range?
(c) attending night school while delivering pizzas (still trying to get that break on off-Broadway)?

Do they: (a) have live-in help?
(b) constantly order gourmet take-out?
(c) eat a lot of pasta?

Will the weekend involve:
(a) additional costs?
(b) interruptions in the hosts' routine?
(c) phobia-inducing situations?

However the comparative analysis comes out, the rules of good behavior require that you make every effort to ensure that your hosts' weekend will be as pleasant as your own. If you are in the same tax bracket, some part of the weekend should be your responsibility. (Offer to take everyone to dinner. Offer to prepare the dinner. Offer to clean up after dinner. Offer to babysit/chauffeur/grocery shop. Remember, their life is still on schedule, it's only yours that is on vacation.) Your presence should not be an inconvenience. Regardless of differences in age or financial status, make arrangements to arrive at their doorstep. If you have a serious food allergy, let them know in advance. A host's prior commitment or unfortunate emergency may interrupt the weekend. Accommodate the plan and do what you can to ease their concerns for your welfare.

If the hosts are always in the "A" category, and you are too, you should simply do what comes naturally. They may offer to pick you up at the airport, but not before you offer to take a cab. Either way, it's a question of convenience. You should offer to take them out for dinner/lunch/brunch, simply to relieve the burden. If the hosts are consistently a "C" and you are embarrassingly enough, still an "A," be thoughtfully generous, but not ostentatiously so. On the other hand, if you are predictably in the "C" grouping and the hosts have been in "A" shape ever since you've known them, be openly appreciative without fawning (it can be done).

House presents

Yes, you should bring one. Put some thought into the gift. What do the hosts do with their leisure time? Golf, garden, cook, read? Try to match your gift with their interests unless, of course, it's watching TV, in which case feel free to present them with something you particularly enjoy and could pass on to them (Nerf football, Ouija board, curiosity about a nearby landmark). At least that way you won't be politely bored the whole time. If you don't know your hosts' interests, arrive with fresh flowers and plan to send something small, but singularly appropriate when you send your thank-you note. Don't overdo it. A creative memento will receive the highest marks, even if it's found at the bottom of a Cracker Jack box.

House manners

Be observant: The rule of thumb is to follow your hosts' lead. When asked, "What time do you like to have breakfast?" assume that you are expected to eat breakfast, most likely with the host, and reply, "What time do you usually have yours?" (Be prepared to set your alarm.) Do they dress for dinner, go to bed early, turn the lights out as they leave the room? Take your cue from them . . . believe us, it's there to be taken.

Be helpful: Offer to run a last-minute errand, babysit for an hour, set the table, pick up the Sunday paper. An hour or two before departure time, ask if you should "strip your bed." This involves taking quilts and blankets off, folding them neatly and putting them aside, and removing the sheets and pillowcases. Depending upon the formality of the household, you may either fold the linens and leave them on top of the blankets (now on the bare mattress or mattress cover) or put the sheets inside a pillowcase along with your towel and facecloth and drop the "bag" off in the laundry basket.

Be self-reliant: If they have a standing tennis match Sundays at 10:00 A.M., assure them that you have a good book, would love to take a walk, were hoping to get a letter off or work on Monday's presentation, and will look for them around noontime. "Not to worry, . . . delighted to have the time."

Be polite: Make sure that you have been introduced (even if it means introducing yourself) to everyone in the household. Shake hands, repeat their names—and whatever other mnemonic devices you find effective. You are everyone's guest, so do what you can to periodically disengage from your fiance's loving gaze and enter into the group activity. Do not leave the table without asking to be excused (they will assume a phone call for you is unexpected and possibly an emergency . . . which is just what the person with whom you left the number should assume). Say "Good morning" at breakfast, and "Good night" before you retire. Praise the cook for a delicious meal, appreciate the view/garden/artwork. The cocktail hour is not the time to delve into a book or last month's issue of *Scientific American*. Be sociable, and always, always, thank your host.

Be entertaining: The invitation sounded so cheery, but on arrival you sense the mood has changed. Do what you can to figure out the source of tension and then give it your best shot. Strike up a monologue with senile Uncle Harry, or take the five-year-old twins out for an exhausting game of sock tag. Humorous intervention from a third party, an invited guest no less, has been known to distract, if not disarm, warring factions. Bad news in the extreme—death in the family, loss of job, appointment of a parole officer—warrants an offer to do your best disappearing act. Genuinely convey your condolences quickly followed by, "I can have a cab pick me up in ten minutes," unless, of course, you are convinced that it really would help if you stayed.

When the invitation is for more than a weekend, keep in mind the haunting adage, "Fish and houseguests begin to smell after three days." At some magical point, perhaps even during the weekend if you visit often, you will cease to be a guest and start to be a member of the family. And at that point, you should begin to assume daily chores. Clear the table, load the dishwasher, etc. "What can I do to help?" is no longer the token gesture it once might have been. (Shame on you.) You've benefited from their routines; now it's time they benefit from you.

Making Your Bed

Making a bed is a lot like wrapping a present, at least the ones that come in boxes. In either case you are trying to make a neatly folded cover out of loose sheets. The trick is in the neatness of the fold. If you have a "fitted" sheet you have a sheet with four elasticized corners. These corners fit snugly around the corners of the mattress, and presto, you have just completed one-third of the exercise. If you do not have a fitted sheet, if both sheets are "flat," you will have to make the corners yourself. Follow the long crease in the center of the sheet. Line it up (length-wise) with the middle of the bed and try to leave an even overhang at both ends. Tuck in the head and foot (the ends) (fig. 1). Standing at one side, pick up the hem or edge of the sheet midway between head and foot and pull it out (tightly) to reach the height of the bed (90°) (fig. 2). Relax the sheet slightly as you continue to pull it up another 180°, letting it rest on top of the bed (fig. 3). Tuck in the triangles below the mattress line (fig. 4). Once again, pick up the point and bring it back down to the original position. Tuck in that triangle (fig. 5). This is what is known as a hospital corner. Do the same on the other side of the bed. For those of you who allow corner-making to preempt common sense, the top sheet needs hospital corners only at the foot of the bed. Is there a blanket? Put it on with the top sheet unless you

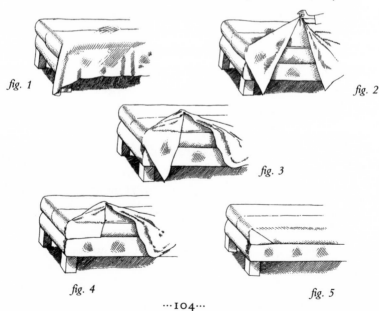

fig. 1

fig. 2

fig. 3

fig. 4

fig. 5

really want the practice. (Why make four corners when you can make two doubles?) Now comes the part that has to do with preference. Do you bring the top sheet and blanket all the way up to the edge of the bed's head, do you bring them up and then fold them back, or do you bring them up, fold them back, and, holding the fold two-thirds of the way over from the side your guest will climb in on, "turn it down"? Should the pillowcase hem face the door or the wall? It's up to you.

Some last-minute words of advice: Don't leave your glass on any wooden surface. Look around for a coaster or even last month's *New Yorker*. You wouldn't want your visit to be remembered by a series of permanent rings on the dining-room table. Similarly, wet towels and bathing suits should not be left to dry on the mahogany bedpost. Leave them to drip dry in the shower.

If you must smoke, do so outside (unless, of course, your host has the same habit and cherishes the company). And just before you leave, make an effort to say good-bye to every member of the household. Your gracious farewell will serve you twice, once to express your thanks in person, and again to keep the weekend's vignettes fresh in your mind for a most thoughtfully written thank-you note.

HOW TO PACK A BAG

❖

We are born into this world with neither emotional nor material baggage. But from the moment the umbilicus is tied off we begin acquiring both. For the first eighteen or twenty years of life, all those cartons and trunks and hatboxes seem to be somebody else's concern and we pay scant attention to any of them. Then, all of a sudden, we find out it's all ours. Friends and family and paid counselors line up to tell us what to do with the emotional baggage—how much of it we have, the best way to pack it, and the most emotionally efficient place to store it—but where are they when we are packing a real bag for a real trip?

There's no great trick to packing a bag—you simply have to know where you're going and for how long. If in doubt as to either of these, and if a spirit of adventure is not something you wish to cultivate, stay home until you have a bit more information. Otherwise, packing a bag will be a riddle with no answer before you set out and a source of recrimination and regret when you get there.

It would be nice if you could pack in such a way as to be prepared for any eventuality, but in the real world this is not possible. There may well be surprises in store for you when you arrive at your destination, but if you've done your homework, they probably won't be the kind of surprises that require a special costume. Even if you had time to change into it.

Duration and destination are the first two givens. The kind of bag you're packing is the third. You pack a soft-sided bag—duffel, carry-on, backpack—somewhat differently from the way you do a standard suitcase. The standard suitcase opens up like a clamshell. The better the suitcase, the more panels and ribbons and pockets its interior has, all designed to prevent the contents from shifting and mixing and approximating the appearance of laundry fresh from the dryer (or, if something has leaked or shattered, not so fresh and ready for the washing machine). It has to be designed this way because the position in which you pack the bag is not always the position in which the bag will travel. If your dress or suit has to look wonderful immediately upon arrival—you're getting married in the suit, you're hoping to sell the dress design to an upscale boutique—a hard-sided bag improves your chances enormously.

A soft-sided bag is likely to have fewer internal restraints. Because its sides and bottom are soft, the contents aren't armored against the shocks that airport baggage handlers and unpaved roads may administer. In its favor, it weighs less unpacked than the Samsonite or the Louis Vuitton, and if you haven't packed your best china in it, it can be stowed in odd nooks and crannies of car trunks and overhead luggage compartments. When not in use it takes up less room in the closet at home. Better yet, the soft-sided bag won't bruise your hip or your shin as you lug it around. Although some hard-sided bags are equipped with wheels, allowing you to trundle them along level surfaces like giant pull toys, not all are. If you're going to be traveling any distance unaided by porters, keep this in mind.

But whether your suitcase is rigid or not, big or small, your object is the same. You want your clothing, toilet articles, shoes, and whatever else you're taking to arrive at your destination looking no worse for their travel experience than you do. Also, you want to keep all of these items separate from one another. That means, don't wrap your shoes in your linen blouse, don't roll up that bottle of shampoo in the gabardine slacks, and don't imagine that life in a suitcase bears any relation to life in a chest of drawers.

Although there are no guarantees in travel, let's hopefully suppose that your duffel bag is going to travel and be carried at the same angle as the one at which you pack it. Bulky, unbreakable, and unyielding items like men's sturdy shoes should go in first. Save space: If you don't use shoe trees, stuff rolled-up socks, tightly coiled belts, or a well-wrapped bottle of ink or scent in the cavity of each shoe. The shoe is also a good place for the spare pair of glasses—in its case, of course—or the tube of lotion or sunscreen, which should be as impermeably wrapped in plastic as the ink bottle. (A cautionary note: Heavy shoes are good for protecting the semi-fragile object. Sandals are not.)

You'll be wearing one pair of shoes, packing a second. Do you need a third? Are you going to jog? Ride a horse? Climb an alp? The special activity may require that you be specially shod. If not, try to imagine yourself getting along on this trip with only two pairs of shoes, both of which you've worn before. Don't tell yourself you'll break in the new ski boots or sandals when you get there; the reverse is more likely to be true.

Since you don't want shoe polish rubbing off on the polo shirt or the buckle of the skirt scratching the finish on your shoes, it will help if you slide the shoes into old wool socks, plastic bags, or the expensive velour baggies that are manufactured for just this purpose. It wouldn't hurt to slide that pile of underwear and sport shirts into a sack, either, the better to organize your bag's interior. The bulky bilingual dictionary and the lacquer box go in this bottom layer, too. A short stack of clothing that can stand to be squashed could go in next to the shoes and piled no higher.

The second layer will contain items you want to pack flat, like skirts and trousers. Unless your carry-on or duffel bag is bigger than any we've ever seen, you're not going to be able to pack them perfectly flat. They'll need to be folded in half, or in thirds in the case of trousers and long skirts. People used to pack with tissue paper; now we pack with plastic. The bags your dry-cleaning comes back in will do, but if you travel all the time, the heavy-duty plastic bags for sale in laundromats are more practical and give greater protection.

If you have items that can't survive a friendly jostle, lay them on this softer layer of fabric and protect them with other soft items—your underwear, for example, or your bathing suit. The uppermost layer will provide protection from the top. Here is the place for your sportscoat or the suit you're not wearing on the travel day. If you've ever had a suit mailed to you from the store, you'll remember how neatly the jacket was folded. You can do the same and, with any luck and if nobody has sat on your bag for long periods of time in very humid weather, it shouldn't look notably worse when it comes out of the bag than when it went in.

Here's how you fold the jacket: With the jacket facing you, put one hand in each shoulder. Turn the left shoulder—but not the sleeve—inside out. Slip the right shoulder inside the left shoulder. The two front halves of the jacket now mirror each other as do the lapels, the inner facing of the jacket is now outside and its sleeves are trapped inside the fold. The material on either side of the jacket's back seam takes care of itself, falling neatly into a half fold the length of the jacket. Now, depending on the dimensions of your bag and the length of your jacket, you can lay it lengthwise along the layer of shirts or blouses, tucking the tip of the collar down at the edge of one pile and the tails down around the edge of the other. Or you can fold it double, which will probably leave room at one end for a toilet kit to be wedged in against one wall and for a rolled up robe and slippers or sandals to go in at the other. Slipping the jacket into a heavy-duty plastic bag before you fold it over may spare your garment a few creases.

Can you pack anything on top of the jacket? You can but you'd do better to leave a little room between the last item packed and the zipper. In the first place, you don't want to offer your bag's zipper challenges it wasn't manufactured to meet. So don't force it. In the second place, although your jacket won't suffocate, you don't want to encourage permanence in creases and folds you hope are merely temporary.

If clothing does come out of your luggage at journey's end looking rumpled, it can be hung in a steam-filled bathroom for a while and the creases will succumb to the same humidity that would have encouraged them when the garment was still packed. (This technique is not good indefinitely. It will work once or twice, but eventually that suit or jacket will have to be pressed.)

Will you be staying long enough at your destination to make unpacking worthwhile or will you be using your bag as your chest of drawers? If the latter is the case, it may be a good idea to pack shirts in one plastic bag, underwear and socks in another, and so forth. Will you be away long enough to produce laundry? You'll want a plastic bag in which to stow it until you can get to a washing machine or until you resign yourself to washing stuff out in the washbasin or the bathtub. An incentive to doing your laundry sooner rather than later will be the space dirty clothes take up in your luggage. Why should dirty clothes take up more room than clean, you may wonder? Travelers down through the ages have scratched their heads over the same question. No one knows why. No one. It may have something to do with wadding being a bulkier way to pack than folding. But it may have to do with greasy molecules all holding their breath to make your life harder. Some seasoned travelers admit to folding their unwashed laundry, the better to pack their bags. We think this is extreme. Simply remember to pack two to three cups of cold-water detergent, double bagged. A short elastic clothesline will come in handy. Do you have sports clothing or a swimsuit that may still be damp when you're ready to pack? More plastic.

What to Pack
Explaining how to pack is relatively easy; because everybody's trip is different, specifying what to pack is presumptuous. That said, here are a few suggestions: If you and the bag are headed for some other country, pack a washcloth and soap. Sample sizes of shampoo, deodorant, and toothpaste save space. A jackknife and a small flashlight may not get used every day, but when you need either one—to cut fruit and cheese at a picnic, to find your glasses when the power goes out at your hotel—you'll be glad you packed it. A button might come loose; take needle and thread.

If you're going to be walking a lot when you get there, experienced pedestrians swear by lambswool. If a toe begins to burn or a sore spot to develop, lambswool gives the trouble spot the cushioning it requires. You get it at the drugstore, not at the farmers' market.

If you're going to be entrusting the bag to a bus or airline company, that is, if you're going to be separated from your bag, you'll want to put tags with your name and address on its outside and on its inside as well. Even with name tags, a bag could get lost but it won't be the end of the world unless it contains irreplaceable items— family photographs, a talisman, this year's journal. So don't pack anything whose loss would spoil your trip or ruin your life.

A jackknife and a twist of lambswool don't add much to your total weight. Neither do a change of bathing suit and a paperback book you've been meaning to read. But everything adds up. Were you traveling by ocean liner, it would all be very simple and you wouldn't have to make any choices. You could just take everything you own. In flea markets or somebody's grandmother's attic, you may have seen something called a steamer trunk. About as big as your chest of drawers and your closet combined, it was built for a people and an era to whom the idea of traveling light never occurred. The contemporary equivalent of this would involve strapping your dresser onto a refrigerator dolly. Since this is not practical, you should think not only about where you're going and what you're going to be doing once you get there, but also about the number of times you're going to have to move your baggage and how. Hitchhiking cross-country dictates one style of packing; driving your own car from the place where you live to your host's front door another. And compromise is possible: You can pack light and return heavy—you're going to Malaysia and know you'll want to stock up on sarongs; you're going to Paris and know you'll want to stock up on books—simply by stuffing a lightweight nylon carryall into one end of your luggage. Halfway through your trip, when you're tired of carrying your purchases in disintegrating paper bags, out comes the carryall. You're better balanced with two pieces of luggage anyway.

The rule of thumb on what to pack and what to leave home comes in two parts. Part one: Take the item if you can't get it where you're going and it could make all the difference between a great trip and merely an okay one: The address book with the name of the friend of a friend; a mosquito repellent if it's going to be buggy; some mild medicine for your stomach if you've got a delicate one and you have reason to believe that danger lurks at the dinner table; a camera, if a trip with no snapshot creates the same quandary for you as a tree falling unheard in the forest does for sophomores in their first philosophy course; special sports equipment.

Rule of thumb, part two: If it's heavy, leave it behind—the trilingual dictionary. Or bulky—the leather trenchcoat. Leave it behind if it's uniquely precious or very fragile. Leave it behind if you aren't sure you'll need it and can get something just as good at only a slight premium where you're going: the extra tube of toothpaste, for example, or the can of tobacco. And if it's going to be a source of worry, don't take it. Here, reality is not the best guide. If you merely fear that security will be bad, you don't want to take your top-of-the-line Walkman; the host country nationals may be as honest as the day is long but anxiety is not always banished by simple facts. If cleaning that silk shirt is always a problem, it will take up as much space in your head as in your luggage and to no greater purpose. Leave it home. How attached are you to the diamond bracelet your mother left you? One way to find out is to take it on a trip and fret about losing it.

HOW TO IRON A SHIRT

❖

You went through college in a T-shirt, you say? Or, you went through college in the snowbelt where people wore flannel shirts from September through May and the shirt you wore to graduation was brand new or just back from the dry cleaners? You've been taking your shirts to the same laundry for so long they've put you on their Christmas-card list, but now they're closed for renovations? Then it's understandable that you never learned to iron a shirt yourself. No one's blaming you. But you do have a job or a social life that occasionally requires a shirt and tie. Or simply that you put in an appearance looking less . . . spontaneous. Just-got-out-of-bed dressing has its place but its place is not everywhere. So here's what to do with a hot iron and a clean but wrinkled shirt.

The shirt we are talking about is made of 100 percent cotton. It's the only shirt worth ironing, or for that matter, wearing. Happily it is today's fabric of fashion, but once there was something called wash-and-wear. Misleading because although you could wash them and wear them, it looked as if that was exactly what you'd done. As if that weren't enough, they were less warm in winter and embarrassingly hot in the summer. Also, even their contemporary equivalents, those polyester–cotton blends, have a tendency to pill. So, buy cotton and learn how to iron.

Presumably you're going to wash the shirt before you iron it. Out of the washing machine and into the dryer is all very well but take care not to fry the shirt. Fried or merely dried, ironing is much easier when the shirt is slightly damp. You can either flick water on it with your fingers or swoop it through the shower and then roll it up in a bath towel or a plastic bag until the material is evenly damp. Or use a spray (the mister you use for your houseplants works well). A word of caution: Damp does not mean soaking wet. When a wet cotton shirt meets with a hot iron there is often an accompanying burning smell followed by a shriek as you separate the two to find a brown imprint of the iron's face grinning up at you. You probably don't have time to wash and dry this shirt a second time, and because that may be your only hope for removing the scorch mark it will be best to put it in the hamper and pull a second shirt from the ironing pile.

To begin: Turn the collar of the shirt up and spread it on the ironing board. Working from the points in toward the midpoint, guiding wrinkles away from the seams with the point of the iron, smooth the collar with the flat of the iron (fig. 1).

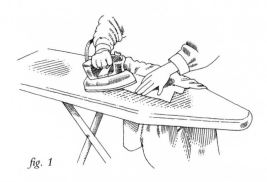

fig. 1

Next, fit one shoulder of the shirt over the nonsquare end of the board. It's as if you were going to dress the ironing board. You're not; you're ironing the yoke of the shirt. Work from one shoulder in toward the center of the back (fig. 2), then switch shoulders and iron the other side of the yoke.

Now iron the sleeves. Spread the cuff open and iron the outside in the same way you did the collar. Then lay the sleeve flat the length of the board, smoothing the

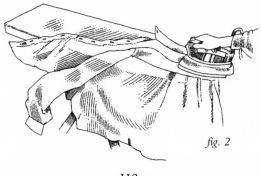

fig. 2

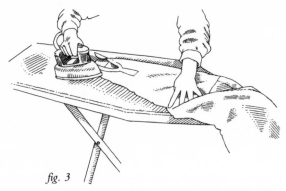

fig. 3

material from the bottom seam toward the top (fig. 3) and making sure there are no wrinkles underneath. No sense in ironing creases into the backside. Repeat the procedure with the second sleeve.

With sleeves, yoke, and collar done, you can now finish the broad, flat, easy surfaces of the shirt . . . commonly known as the back and front. Fit one shoulder over a corner of the board's squared end and smooth that half of the shirtfront out along the board. Iron along the placket and around the pocket. Iron the placket and the pocket. Slide the shirt across the board so that the newly ironed portion is hanging free and you have the back of the shirt uppermost. Iron that. Now do the other half of the shirtfront.

Put the shirt on a hanger, button the top button, and hang it someplace like the shower rack or your chinning bar so it will dry completely. If you jam it into your closet at this point, it will assume a new set of wrinkles and eventually need to be ironed again. If, on the other hand, you have to wear it RIGHT NOW, take a deep breath (the shirt will feel cold—that's bad, but it only makes you stand up straighter—that's good). Because the idea is to keep the ironed shirt from drying into wrinkles, you can try to form-fit its front to your torso by holding the ends of the two side seams between your thumbs and index fingers, pulling those ends straight out from the sides and then behind you to meet in the center of your back. The front will keep remarkably wrinkle-free, and the back . . . the back? If you're planning to wear a jacket and you're really in a tear—and planning not to remove it—you needn't bother to iron the back of the shirt.

It's obvious, isn't it, why it's just as easy to iron five shirts as one. It takes time to set up the ironing board, it takes time to heat the iron—about two minutes. You might as well do all five and get them out of the way. That's five times you won't have to wonder if you have a clean, ironed shirt. No ironing board? A bath towel spread flat on a table or a desk will have to do. No iron? You can always take a soaking wet shirt, smooth out the wrinkles as best you can, and hang it up to literally drip-dry in the shower. If it's pima cotton and your bathroom is reasonably dry, within twelve hours you'll probably have a shirt dry enough and barely respectable enough to wear. But this is an emergency measure when you have twelve hours before the emergency itself is scheduled. Wouldn't it be better to buy an iron?

HOW TO WRAP
A PRESENT

❖

For the sake of instruction, let's put the cart before the horse. Let's assume that you have thought long and hard and finally come up with The Most Perfect Present. You are so pleased with your idea that it makes you smile just to think about it. You can't wait to see everyone's face when it is opened. It's going to make you a star. So, you've thought of it, you've bought it, and now it's time to take it home and wrap it. In the words of the immortal Captain Hook, "Here's where the canker g-naws." Not for lack of the card shop's variety of paper and ribbon, not for an unfamiliarity with tape and scissors, it's just that whenever you try to do it, the package comes out looking as if you sat on it.

Nature's most perfect package is the eggshell. It is sleek, it is smooth, and it carries its contents with the greatest care. For a novice gift-wrapper, the most perfect package begins with a box. Its durability provides safe passage for the gift and its uniformity facilitates the decoration, which, in this case, is wrapping paper. Blessed are the frugal, for they are the ones who insist on saving the wrapping paper from year to year (carefully teasing the tape from the paper so as not to remove the design and leave a white blotch, turning a simple bridal shower into a veritable monsoon). If this is a tradition in your family, you have probably never seen a virgin piece of wrapping paper, one without wrinkles and tears. Predictably, when you are miles away from home, living on your own, the act of purchasing a clean, smooth roll of wrapping paper may send you straight to confession, in which case you should call home and ask for an early installment on your portion of the family's heirlooms. The practice of recycling wrapping paper is laudable. However, for purposes of instruction, because the object is to enhance the gift with a smooth presentation, we will assume that the paper you are using is fresh. (You can cut costs, time, and environmental concerns with a purchase of plain white tissue paper, and two yards of cloth ribbon—no one throws real ribbon away.)

Now you have a box, paper, and ribbon. You need a clean, hard surface to work on (a table, the counter, or

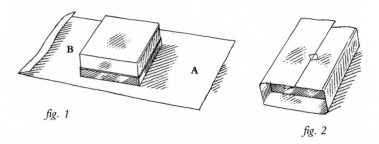

fig. 1

fig. 2

the floor—not the bed), a pair of scissors, and a roll of tape. Unfold a double sheet of tissue paper or a single piece of heavy paper, design side down, on the table and put the box on top of the paper. The paper should be long enough to overlap by 2" when side A is brought up to meet side B (fig. 1), and wide enough to be two-thirds the height of either side. Cut the paper to fit. Put the gift into the box and gently tape the box closed. Tape side A to the bottom of the box. Roll the box toward side B, making sure that the paper is tight and even. Make a fold (a hem, if you will) along side B, hiding inside what may be a ragged edge from a hasty cutting job with very dull scissors. Put the nice, neat, folded edge of side B over side A and tape it (fig. 2). Now for the ends—let's name them 1, 2, 3, and 4. As you push 1 down and in to meet the box (fig. 3), 2 and 4 will change from rectangles into triangles (or, more precisely, from a horizontal projection to a diagonal projection). Fold 2 and 4 toward the center, making sure that the

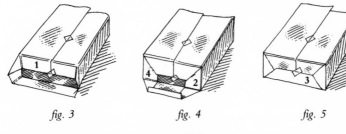

fig. 3   *fig. 4*   *fig. 5*

crease along the box is without wrinkles (fig. 4). It should be looking more and more like an envelope. Before you bring 3 up to cover 2 and 4 and be taped to 1 (fig. 5), fold over the multiple edges, making one neat edge. Just look at the diagram, it's not as difficult as it sounds.

The length of the ribbon should equal the perimeter of the length and width of the box plus an additional amount for the bow. Put the wrapped box on the table, bottom (seam) side down. Put the middle of the ribbon in the middle of the box and run it along the length of the box. Bring it down over both sides. Then lift the box as you continue to bring the two ends of ribbon toward the middle of the bottom of the box. Turn the box over. With equal tension on both ends, cross one end over the other at the middle of the box. Assuming you have crossed the right end over the left, think of the two ribbon ends as hands on a clock . . . it is now 9:15 (fig. 6). Now turn the clock back (fig. 7), moving the hands (ribbon ends) to read 6:00. Continue taking the ends around

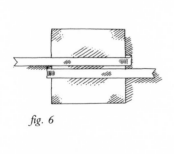

fig. 6

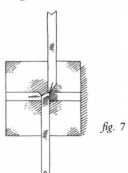

fig. 7

the sides of the box and returning them to the top of the box. Make a basic knot. Make a simple bow. If you grew up with Velcro sneakers and digital watches, take a closer look at the diagram, make a knot, cut the ends, and buy a matching stick-on bow. Or use pre-tied gold or silver elastic ties. There are so many ways to avoid the basics. But our advice is to master them.

Of course, there are limitations to the box and paper with ribbon approach. The bigger the gift, the bigger the box, the more paper . . . Refrigerator? Spray paint or funny papers will cover the box, but a nicely wrapped ice-cube tray will do. A complete and utter lack of boxes, an oddly shaped container, or anything that is very long, very sharp, very irregular, may pose a problem. Cylinders can be treated with a series of tucks made on a diagonal roll. A sphere can be given an initial seam and two ends, to resemble the firecracker party favors one dreaded at birthday parties, or you can place the sphere in the center of a square of paper and pull the four corners up, gathering the excess at the top of the sphere and tying it up. If there are sharp edges, wrap the gift in layers of newspaper first. Learning to cope with the irregular may eventually encourage a more creative treatment of the sadly predictable. The tie box may have provided initial relief from novice wrapping anxiety, but it makes the gift so, well, to be truthful, boring.

Worse than boring, it begins to feel that very little thought went into the gift, and the recipient begins to wonder, "Why did Aunt Lyla bother?" At this point we offer a small coda: If a gift is merely *a token* of your esteem, it should reflect just that. Of course there are variables that we are dying to discuss, but the underlying principle is to match your thoughts of gratitude, devotion, loyalty, respect (or any combination therein thereof), with the gift. Once satisfied, we can move on to the variables. Are we marking a weekend at your roommate's parents' country house? The third month of a wild romance that you're hoping he is hoping will last a lifetime? The Intern Program Director's fortieth birthday? Your grandmother's eightieth? Your favorite niece's wedding? On a scale of one to ten, with ten reading "very well" and one reading "hardly at all," ask first, "How well do I know this person?" and then ask, "How significant is the event?" If your score is more than ten, you should find out what the current balance is on your checking account, and if it is lower than you imagined it to be, consider spending in time what you might have spent in dollars making, repairing, orchestrating, or composing your gift. Perhaps there is enough time to take that class at the local university extension service and actually make a quilt for Audrey and her intended, or to paint a watercolor from Grandma's favorite porch, or to polish up the eight sterling dessert spoons Grandma gave to you long ago, and have the jeweler engrave Audrey's initials and wedding date on the backs. Even if your checking account is remarkably healthy, remember, all the money in the world can as easily purchase a thoughtless dud as it can the most appropriate gem.

And what if your score falls below ten? You hardly know the man? Or it is, after all, only a weekend; what should you bring? Consumable goods—wine, soap, candles—are always appreciated, even by the already-owners-of-everything. If you've gone to the trouble to find out personal preferences—Havanas, fresh raspberries, piccalilli—you'll be on your way toward winning a heart.

One final note: don't be afraid to mark the moment. Inscribe the book, engrave the frame, embroider initials and a date on the bandanna. As these objects are used and borrowed and used again, the moment will continue to be remembered.

HOW TO CARVE
A TURKEY

❖

The imagined scenario goes something like this. You're invited to Sunday dinner or Thanksgiving. It could be to a friend's house, it could be to the home of your older sister, or to the apartment of someone you know from work. Either because Thanksgiving is a special occasion and turkey is the appropriate ritual food or because your visit makes the meal a special occasion, a fowl, large or small, has been roasted. Traditionally, the man of the house was expected to carve and serve that bird. Nowadays, not every house has a man in it and the phrase itself—"the man of the house"—is used ironically as often as not. There may still be a man permanently in the house or there may not. There may be two men. The man may have been called away just as you're all supposed to sit down to dinner. But, present or absent, notional or real, none of these men may know how to carve. Amid the last minute flurry in the kitchen, the cry, friendly or desperate, will be heard above the rattle of dishes and the plop of dropped squash, "Does anyone know how to carve?"

This is your opportunity to be a social hero or heroine

and save the day. "I do," you answer. "Now, if I could just sharpen that knife." Before you make this request, however, prepare yourself to be disappointed and to conceal that disappointment. If you know how to carve, you know that a dull knife is a tool of the devil. Your friends' knife may be dull. If it is and your hosts have no sharpening "steel"—a rod of rough-surfaced steel fitted into a handle, a cylindrical file, if you will—you're just going to have to do the job with a less-than-ideal knife. If they do have such a tool, you need to know how to use it.

Grasp the steel in one hand, pointing it at a 45° angle, down and away from your body. Take the carving knife in the other hand and draw it up along the steel toward yourself with the blade at a slight angle to the steel. Then turning your wrist, rest the opposite side of the blade

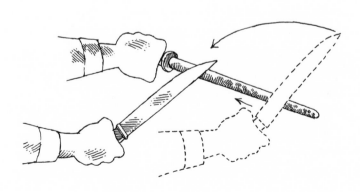

against the steel, and draw the knife up toward yourself again, maintaining the blade at the same slight angle to the steel. Repeat. Think of a grasshopper rubbing its legs together. Repeat and repeat and repeat. Soon the knife will be as sharp as a razor and you will be able to set the same bad example, in demonstration of that fact, that your father would have if he had taught you how to sharpen a knife—shaving a little patch of skin on your forearm, slicing a sheet of paper, making a horizontal groove in your thumbnail. If the knife you've just sharpened is not yours—now, if, indeed, you are playing hero or heroine in someone else's kitchen—it might be thoughtful as well as prudent to warn your hosts that they now have a *sharp* knife.

In the meantime, the bird is cooling. It should have been out of the oven for about twenty minutes, allowing it to collect itself. (This will facilitate the carving. Attempting to carve a piping-hot fowl, just out of the oven, will produce a platter of something that looks more like linguine than sliced white meat.) Before you begin, ask if the carving is to be done at the table, or if the preference is to present a platter of carved meat. Then, roll up your sleeves, tuck in your pearls/tie, and do what you can to protect your front. You might ask for a wet dish towel to keep your hands from becoming too greasy. The first part of carving, removing the legs and wings, is quite physical—something akin to lightweight wrestling—and should be done in the kitchen.

Place the bird on a platter or cutting board, breast side up. Ask for a second, empty platter. If you're right-handed, you'll want the neck of the bird to your left. Plant the carving fork—a two-tined, long handled affair—astride the breast. Cut at the thigh joint nearest to you by pressing the leg away from the body with your left hand and doing what you can to locate the actual joint and severing the ligaments that keep it in place with the point of the knife. Do the same with the wing. The wing can be set aside, but the dark meat from the thigh

and leg should be sliced as neatly as possible (and it's nigh on to impossible to do this neatly). The dark meat should be first on the platter simply because the meat is more moist and able to withstand some exposure to the air.

If the carving is to be done at the table, this is the time for you to restore your impeccable appearance: wash your hands, unroll your sleeves, straighten your tie (or pull out your pearls), and announce that the carver is ready to proceed. If it hasn't already been done for you, remove the high-tech plastic meat thermometer most poultry farms feel compelled to insert. At the table, or in the kitchen, the next step is to carve the white meat. It does tend to dry out, and ideally you will be carving each slice as it is requested at the table. "Duncan, would you like dark meat or white meat?" you ask, and carve or serve from the platter depending upon the response. If all the carving is to be done in the kitchen, slice only enough white meat for the first serving (reassuring the host or hostess that you will be happy to return to the kitchen and produce "seconds"—then do pay attention to the supply, and make good on your offer). Cut thin slices of white meat, working at an angle from the tip of the breastbone down toward the joint where the wing was removed.

No wonder this opportunity isn't more readily seized—it's a real chore! Fortunately everyone recognizes it to be just that, and you will be all the more appreciated for your efforts. Practice makes perfect, but don't go overboard. You're not expected to turn your own place into a test kitchen, buying, roasting, and carving large fowl until you perfect your technique. Tying a bow tie you can practice until your patience runs out. In carving a turkey, you learn as the occasion presents itself.

HOW TO PROPOSE
A TOAST

❖

Time was when there were rules for everything and you could look them up in a book. Now it's not so easy. There are certain occasions—rehearsal dinners, wedding luncheons, diplomatic receptions—where custom dictates who shall offer a toast and when. Far more numerous are the occasions when some milestone is being celebrated, some friend or relative is having a birthday and a toast seems to be called for. If you've organized the party or assembled the friends at the corner bar, it's easy enough to choose the moment. When as many people as you can reasonably expect to show have done so, and before people have begun to leave, you discreetly but firmly call the gathering to attention and propose your toast: "To Maria, may she have as much success as a deputy coroner as she's had in the pathology lab." "To David, congratulations on finishing the boat ahead of schedule and under budget. Anchors aweigh." And so forth. Toasts you anticipate are toasts you can think about and rehearse. The only rules are that they be short, to the point and, whenever possible, sincere.

Toast rhymes with roast. Just as we're no longer

banned from discussing religion, politics, or money at the dinner table—of course, we do so at our peril as conversation is likely to be both livelier and more dangerous—jokes, gentle teasing, and outright insult find their way into toasts. A bachelor dinner almost demands it. (Why? Because one of the ways American men show their affection for one another is by trading insults. Anthropologists call this a "joking relationship.") If you must, joke away. But remember that you're not a stand-up comedian or the national correspondent for a supermarket tabloid. The only rule of thumb here is that the toast be inspired by affection. Also, you don't want things to turn nasty—now or later or ever. So be entertaining, if you can, but be careful.

Now consider a third situation. You're not the host and you yourself are not the birthday girl. You've been invited to a dinner or a gathering, everyone is in good, if unfocused, spirits and you wait for someone to say something. No one does. Perhaps some key moment is being celebrated—a promotion, a housewarming, a party after a christening, Thanksgiving—and although you all know why you're there, you begin to get the uneasy feeling that no one is going to acknowledge the occasion with a toast. If you're sensitive enough to feel this passing opportunity, you probably have the presence of mind to do something about it. If you're at a dinner, a good time to relieve your anxiety would be early on, before everyone has gotten into their conversations. Or, if you have been waiting for someone else to do it and your hopes have remained just that, you'll have a second chance before people dive into the dessert. You raise your glass—we're assuming there's wine in the glass, it could just as well be seltzer water or apple cider, but it must be something (no empty toasts, please)—and say you'd just like to propose a toast to your host or hostess, that it's a pleasure to be with such good friends or, if they aren't, in such good company.

If the gathering isn't organized in space by a table and in time by courses, choosing your moment will be a little trickier. Is everyone there? You don't know because it's not your party. If you know whose party it is, and you probably do, otherwise you wouldn't be concerned about its details, it wouldn't hurt to ask him or her whether or not they were considering making a toast. If such a blatant nudge gets a bland reply like, "Huh?" or, "I just don't know what to say," you can relax. You do know what to say. "Hear, hear," you say, tapping your glass with a spoon, "We all know we're here to celebrate Mary and Joe's new baby. But we'd also like to thank our Office Manager for having had the good idea of getting us together. A toast." Clink. You've done your duty and made your corner of society a better place—temporarily at least—by so doing.

Caveat: If you're the one being toasted—that is, if it's your skills as a cook or virtues as a brother-in-law or prospects as a vice-president in charge of credit that are being toasted, you smile, you express your thanks, but you don't drink the toast with everyone else. That would be like clapping for yourself when you've been awarded first prize or the blue ribbon. And yes, it's true, in what used to be the Soviet Union, they do clap for themselves—they also spend whole evenings toasting each other in descending hierarchical order, from senior guest down to the most junior guest. Think about that the next time you start to drink to your own health.

Second caveat: Along the lines of waiting until everyone has been served, and the hostess has taken the first bite, there is a lesser-known tradition pertaining to the wine at a dinner party organized with no particular celebrity or cause in mind. The rule goes like this. The wine is poured, a toast is proposed by your host or hostess, glasses are raised, and the crystal rings. Then and only then may you drink from your glass. It is not difficult to determine whether or not your host/hostess lives by this tradition. As with all table manners, follow the lead they give. If they allow themselves a sip of wine before offering a toast, you have every reason to follow suit. However, should they begin by making a toast, "To welcome our distinguished guest," you could offer a second toast, "in honor of their generous hospitality." Then you may pursue the perenially absorbing subject of the Elgin Marbles' rightful ownership or who's responsible for the Red Sox's disappointing season.

Third caveat: There seems to be some unexamined custom according to which men offer toasts and, at least in a mixed gathering, women do not. If this didn't go out with tail fins on American sedans, it must have disappeared by the time of the ERA initiative. Anyone can express a group's gratitude or pride. Anyone can attest to a friend's good qualities or bright future.

HOW TO ENTERTAIN
A CHILD

❖

"**B**e Prepared" is the Boy Scouts' marching song. It's the leitmotif of this book and it should be your theme song, too. Be prepared, for example, to entertain someone else's child. You never know when the opportunity will strike: You've gone to call on a friend. The two of you have chosen lemonade and cookies on the patio over a mild rumble brewing in the kitchen. A conversation that is coming deliciously close to revealing her lover's identity, the meaning of life, or one mother's burden is abruptly interrupted by a scream that begins in the pantry, continues down the hall, and carries through the patio door. Your friend wonders, "What's going on?" and you wonder, "Did Dopler have young children?" The sight of blood is all the prompting you need, and so *of course* you will stay with the other children while she takes Jesse to the ER. That's the I-should-be-back-in-an-hour-just-don't-let-them-leave-the-house case.

Opportunity may knock in a less dramatic way and you may not have to rise to the occasion quite so suddenly. Your brother, happily separated from your sister-in-law but determined to maintain his relationship with their children, has Lulu and Buzzy every other weekend. You've flown in for a visit. Big brother meets you at the airport, wearing his Pop-can-I-borrow-the-car grin and you wonder what's up. He picks up your bag, puts his arm over your shoulder, and says, "How would you like to help your brother out of a jam?" The story unfolds. He knew you were coming, even had tickets for tonight's game, but he forgot this was HIS weekend—you vaguely remember telling him that's why you were coming in the first place—and last night this very interesting woman who works at the office asked if he wanted to go to the Beach Boys' concert. Man, you know how much he loves the Beach Boys, he couldn't say no. So, would you be willing to take the kids out for a hamburger and sort of keep them busy for a couple of hours? They think their uncle hung the moon so, really, anything you do will be great. Thanks a million.

A third scenario: It's a family outing and although you're related to no one in the car, passengers under ten years of age have been encouraged to call you Aunt Edie or Uncle Wally. Presuming on this fictive kinship, your friends, their parents, stop at a flea market—you've been to flea markets before and don't like the tenth one any better than you did the first—so you graciously agree to keep an eye on the kids while your friends continue their never-ending quest for Fiestaware.

Did you hang the moon? Do you display grace under pressure? Entertaining someone else's children is a good way to find out. First, let's consider the variables: How well do you know the child or children? How many of them are there? What ages? And what's the occasion? If the sibling has just been rushed to the emergency room, you can bet the child you've volunteered to entertain will be in a different frame of mind from the ones who have a favorite aunt or uncle all to themselves for a whole evening. And what's your own frame of mind? Comfortable with children? Slightly phobic? Children are different from adults, no doubt about it, but some of the ground rules are the same: be polite to the child; be considerate. Entertaining him or her for a few minutes or a few hours may look to you like a problem to be solved. Little Lulu or Buzzy may have a rather different take on it: "Oh, good, a familiar adult all to myself." Or, "Oh, no, where's Mom?" Your charge may be no more articulate about what's on his or her mind than an adult is, so don't treat him like the passive patron of a dinner theater. Think of your temporary stint as babysitter improv, take your cues from the audience.

Let's look at the first scenario first, the one involving—how to put it?—family drama. Your friend and

Jesse have rushed off to the doctor's; the baby is still napping and is most likely to continue regardless of his sister's screams. Young babies, fascinating as they are, are not your best audiences. They need to be fed, they need to be changed, they need to be held, but they do not need to be entertained. Babies are never bored. You might as well try to entertain a cat. Diversion is possible, so is play—entertainment is beyond their ken.

The three-year-old, in contrast, is scared out of his wits. He'd been told to stay out of the kitchen drawer, but he never believed anything in it could really make blood! Your first task is to calm him down by minimizing the trauma. Quickly clean up the crime site as you quietly reassure your new friend that you know it was an accident, that it wasn't anybody's fault, so we'll clean up this mess while Mommy takes Jesse to the doctor and think of something to do.

You're housebound, remember, because the baby's asleep upstairs and there's probably been enough excitement for the moment. Favorite toys, books, and blankets will work for a short time but as the hour can easily stretch into two or three, it would be well to have a few other resources to draw on. Good as you are at making faces, they aren't going to hold the child's attention for more than a couple of minutes. Wiggling your ears may buy you a bit more time, but a project is what's called for. How about a paper hat? You can choose between the standard Commodore's Hat, which is easy to fold and hard to keep on, or the Printer's Cap, recommended by its simple classic lines and utilitarian virtues—pressmen used them to protect their heads from ink dust in the early days of offset printing. It's marginally harder to fold but it's less likely to fall off. Here's how:

Printer's cap

1. Place a full-sized folded newspaper page on a table, open edge toward you. Turn down upper corners to meet at center.
2. Fold lower edge of the top sheet up to base of the triangle.
3. Now fold top sheet over again at base of the triangle. Leave the lower sheet unfolded.
4. Turn the whole thing over and fold the sides in to the center, so that the edges meet.

1

2

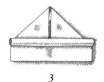

3

5. Fold up corners of the lower edge, forming a small triangle.

6. Fold lower triangle up.

7. Fold the top of the small triangle down and tuck it behind the "band."

8. Turn paper over again and fold point down to bottom edge.

9. Tuck point into band.

10. Open the cap by bringing the lower corners of cap together at center, forming a flat square.

11. Fold closed corners toward center, tucking them under the band.

12. Fold top and bottom corners to meet at center. Cap is now ready to be opened and worn.

The hats can be decorated with color patches cut from discarded magazines—this is for the fourth hour—or crayons and markers. Three-year-olds are tremendously resourceful and know where most things are, even when they're officially "hidden." Supplies are there if you ask for them. When the baby wakes up, be honest and admit to the three-year-old that you've never changed a diaper before. He's seen it done a hundred times and can give you pointers. The more helpless you appear to be, the more responsibility the toddler will assume. If you play your cards right, you can put the newspaper and tape away and, "Do you know how to work this stroller? Should I feed her now? Does Baby like cat food?"—this grownup is so silly—will become the best game in town.

What else can you do with a young child? It all depends: Do you want to tire them out or calm them down? Wild giggling can turn into heartbroken sobs in a trice so before you begin swinging your charges around

10

11

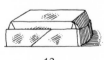

12

by their arms or tossing the younger ones up in the air, consider what shape you and your back are in and how recently the children have had lunch. Perhaps more faces and a spell of wiggling your ears would be more prudent. Or shadow puppets. The handkerchief transformed into a hand puppet may work, provided you have a clean handkerchief.

You can make a real hand puppet by applying lipstick or something easier to wash off to the side of your index finger from the second joint down to where it meets the base of the thumb and around to the first joint of the thumb. Now press side of thumb flat against the metacarpal and, voilà, it's a mouth! A badly made-up, not very pretty mouth, but a mouth all the same. You can add eyes if you want and try to engage the child-to-be-entertained in a conversation. If this fails, draw faces on your knees or on your charges' knees and goof on that for a while—remembering to avoid the indelible markers that don't magically wash off. (Chalk, watercolors, or chocolate pudding works well; ballpoint, gentian violet, or nail polish doesn't.)

How about the older children? Let's get back to Lulu and Buzzy, the niece and nephew you've inherited for the evening. The simple, stupid solution is to sit them in front of a television set or a VCR, thereby doing your own small part for the cretinization of America. Electronic babysitting is not all bad and if you were the child's mother or father, you'd be entitled to the break TV guarantees. But that's not the case with you, is it? Perhaps, this being a temporary assignment, you can do a little bit better. Their father said you could take them out for a hamburger but discussions on who likes what can go on forever, degenerating quickly into a battlefield of "I hate it, yuck" vs. "I love it, please, please." Endless deliberations about where to have dinner are no more interesting with children than they are with adults, so make short work of them by coming up with a two-part plan: We'll get sandwiches at X (naming the restaurant), and then we'll do something really fun. So, quickly, what's really fun in the neighborhood? Is there a playground nearby? Can you find some stale bread to take to the duck pond? How about camping out? Or S'mores?

S'mores have two outstanding qualities. The first has to do with the amount of sugar you are actually allowing the children to consume. The second, and more attractive, has to do with the preparation. S'mores' potential for the kind of mess children love and adults can live with is high. A further recommendation is that they require some sort of fire, and it can take most of the night. A fireplace, a charcoal grill, or a camp fire will do nicely. The ingredients? If your brother has the kids every other weekend, he may already have them on hand: marshmallows, chocolate bars (Hershey's Milk Chocolate without almonds is the popular favorite), and graham crackers.

You'll also need to locate long-handled forks. Your brother probably didn't get them when the marital property was divided, so you may have to make a detour to the hardware store. Were you wondering what to bring as a house present? Stop wondering—these are perfect. If you already have a house present and there is no hardware store, he must be living in the country. Long green twigs, cut from volunteer brush, work well. The kids can help to strip the bark. ("No whipping, guys, and I don't want to have to tell you again . . .") Straightened coat hangers and fishing rods don't work at all and neither do table forks. What you're aiming for is length—providing distance from direct heat—and a wooden handle. Once you've located the cooking implements and got the fire going, the rest is easy.

Toast the marshmallow. Make a sandwich with the toasted marshmallow, half a chocolate bar, and two graham crackers. Kids love 'em. There is a serious downside to this epicurean distraction. Aside from sticky hands and the potential for tummy aches—"You saw your brother eat how many?"—you will surely have increased your charges' energy level just when you were hoping to move on to brushing teeth and getting into pajamas. What about a quick game of sock tag? Sock tag, precursor of Nerf, can be played anywhere, with variations to accommodate age and ability. All you need is a pair of socks. Players are free to run through the house (or around the outside).

The rules are simple: you are "it" if you are hit by the sockball. You are no longer "it" once you have successfully tagged another player with the sockball. It's a good idea to designate "free zones" (a chair or corner where a player can rest without fear of being hit). Only one player per zone, the number of players should exceed the number of zones by two. Do what you can for safety—close off the stairs, clear the kitchen counter of glassware, put the table lamps in the closet and don't let the game go on too long.

If it was mentioned, niece or nephew will remember that, "You promised we could go camping!" Does their father have a tent? Set it up in the living room (use chair legs as stakes, weight the chair with books if it slides). No tent? Use a sheet. You don't need sleeping bags when you can make honest-to-God bedrolls the way the cowpokes did. A blanket with a sheet on top, folded in half and in half again, rolled up and tied with a belt, that's authentic! Now's the time to tell a story about the adventures with their father, you were just about their ages, yes, that's right, decided to go into the lumber business and cut down the neighbor's ornamental cherry tree. What he said. What you said. What their father said. Keep it up, you're doing fine. They'll be asleep in no time.

Whew! Desperate and a bit ground down by all this expense of imagination and energy, won't you be glad to see Mom or Dad walk through the door! "Sorry," they say, "we had to wait," or, "the traffic leaving the concert was unbelievable. But we knew the kids would be okay with you." "No problem," you reply. "Glad to do it. We all got along just fine."

HOW TO REPLACE
A PANE OF GLASS

❖

So you've decided to take up juggling, and your sweetie sent you a set of Indian clubs. Or you got tired of the rain and thought the front hallway was big enough for a little one-on-one soccer. Maybe you think your landlord does read the fine print and you suspect you've already run through the damage deposit six times. "Why did you do that?" or "How did that happen?" have always seemed irrelevant questions surrounding every genuine accident from spilt milk to broken windows. Anyone knows the more relevant question should be, "Can you fix it?" If the answer is yes, you are in luck. Spilled milk requires a sponge, water, and apologies. The broken window takes a bit more work to repair, but in the process you will amaze your friends and gain a tremendous sense of satisfaction knowing (a) the window is fixed and (b) your skill has forestalled predictable ire. Here's how:

You will need: a tape measure, a hammer, a standard (flat-head) screwdriver, a piece of sandpaper, a small can of exterior (latex water-based) paint, a sash brush, a putty knife, ten glazier's points (don't worry, that's what they are called), a small can of glazing compound, and a pane of glass. It's all available at the hardware store with the possible exception of the glass, which you can get at the glass store (look in the yellow pages, they will cut it to size if you ask).

It may be much warmer inside, and God knows the footing is better, but replacing a broken pane of glass is done from the outside. Put on your warm jacket, a hat, scarf, and workgloves, if you have them, and make sure the ladder is being held by a strong and reliable friend.

First, remove the broken glass *carefully*—it cuts! and put it in your glass recycle container. Next, remove the old putty and glazier's points from the frame by using the screwdriver to pry, crack, coax, doing your best not to gouge the wood. Fold the sandpaper into a 2" x 3" rectangle, making a stiff edge to work with, and gently sand the groove so that it is relatively smooth and clear of any old putty and dirt.

Mix a small amount of paint with an even smaller amount of water in a jar or can. Using the sash brush, paint the surface you have just sanded so that the wood is sealed. This seems like a step you could skip, but be assured, if you do, the oil in the glazing compound will sink into the unpainted wood and leave the compound to harden and crack, allowing the pane to loosen before the lease is up. As soon as the paint is dry, the frame is ready for the glass. Measure the size of the rectangle formed by the frame (and write the measurements down), and then cut a piece of cardboard to tape over the opening while you go to the glass store for the new piece of glass. You might want to call in advance and ask if they will custom cut the piece (most will, but it's a pain when you find yourself in the one that won't). The measurement to ask for should be ⅛" in length and width LESS than the actual frame opening (wooden frames are not always exactly even, and that ⅛" will give you some margin for error plus natural expansion/contraction).

Now you are back at the site, the frame has been primed, and you are ready to use the screwdriver to pry open the can of glazing compound and the putty knife to spread a thin layer of compound along the four sides of the frame. (Do use a putty knife—experience shows that an old table or kitchen knife doesn't have the straight edge of a putty knife and won't do as good a job, plus putty knives are relatively cheap, and if kept clean, they last.) Get the glazier's points out and put them within easy reach. Press the glass onto the puttied frame (it should stay in place), and using your screwdriver and hammer tap the points halfway into the wooden frame, spaced evenly, roughly three inches apart.

Once the pane is secured by the points, take a hunk of

glazing compound out of the can and roll it between your hands to form a snake (½" to ¼" thick). Put the snake all along the edge of the glass and then press it with the putty knife to form an angled edge from the glass to the outside of the frame. Read the directions on the compound container to find out how long you will need to wait for it to dry before painting (it may be a week or a season depending upon where you live and what time of year it is when the window breaks). Because of the time required between the next to last and the last step, it is a good idea to thoroughly clean the brush and to leave it on top of the can of paint in a place that you will see from time to time (i.e., above the television, on the kitchen counter, or in the front hallway). It will serve as a reminder of the almost-finished status of your otherwise fabulous repair job.

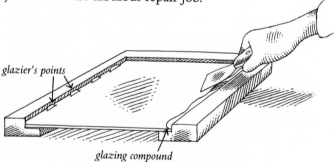

glazier's points

glazing compound

HOW TO UNCLOG A DRAIN
(with advice on how to retrieve an heirloom from the trap)

❖

This chapter is included for two reasons. The first, and more frequent, reason is to remedy a clogged drain. The second, and more desperate, reason is to retrieve a priceless diamond earring that you borrowed from your friend's mother that slipped from between your trembling fingers as you were leaning over the sink, trying to get just a little closer to the mirror and saying to yourself, "I sure hope I don't lose these." If you find yourself in this second category, take a deep breath, relax, and skip to page 161.

The clogged drain may be in the sink or the bath/shower. Rarely does this happen instantaneously. It is likely that the water has been leaving the tub more and more slowly each day. Being optimistic, you hoped that whatever it was that was holding things up would work itself out. (This is the same sort of approach some parents take toward adolescence.) At any rate, an overnight guest or an impatient roommate will no doubt encourage you to come up with a more aggressive solution. *Don't* call the plumber just yet. You need an adjustable wrench (they are very handy and you only need to buy one in your lifetime, unless you lend it out regularly, in which case a name tag is a good idea), a plumber's helper (a great housewarming present), a jar of petroleum jelly (Vaseline), and maybe some chemical drain cleaner. Unless you are thinking of going into the plumbing business, you don't need to buy the most expensive adjustable wrench. As for the plumber's helper (sometimes called a plunger), you should look for one that has a wide, flat-rimmed opening like a bell, not one that looks like a muted trumpet.

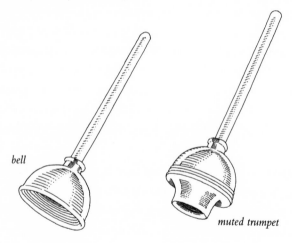

bell

muted trumpet

If this is a clogged bathroom sink, there may be a stopper in your way. Remove the stopper by turning it counterclockwise and lifting it out of the drainpipe. Older sinks depend on a crossbar rather than a stopper, and since it can't be removed, you'll have to ignore it. In a tub, if there is a chrome disk with holes placed over the drain (held in place with a single screw), remove it with a screwdriver. The object is to pull the blockage back up into the sink or tub by creating a vacuum, so you need a clear shot. This isn't pretty, but it works, and it saves the plumber from having to charge you an arm and a leg when he finally fits your sink into his schedule some time next week. Brace yourself, and rest assured that you will gain both personal satisfaction and a functional sink.

Push an old washcloth or corner of a towel into the hole above the drain (it's called the overflow) to more or less seal it off. There may be water in the sink already. If not, turn on the water and draw about one or two inches into the bowl. Put a coating of petroleum jelly on the rim of the plunger (supposedly this makes for a better seal, but if you don't have any on hand, don't worry about it, this step is optional). Put the plunger over the drain hole at an angle and do your best to force out what little air there is in the plunger's chamber. At this point the plunger should be as flat as possible against the bottom of the sink. Of course you should read and even rehearse this paragraph so that you don't need to read as you work. It's really quite simple. You are trying to build up enough force within the pipe to dislodge the goop that is plugging up the sink. Keeping the suction cup in place, pull up and push down on the handle several times and then pull the handle and cup all the way up and out of the sink. Ta dah! Did you get it? No? Well, try again. Try two or three more times.

Water still sitting in the sink? Now is the time to try using a coat hanger, which you have straightened for this eventuality. You may be able to nudge the blockage just enough to return with the plunger and finish the job. If that doesn't work, and you are now determined to see this thing through (as it were), you can try using a garden hose with or without water. This seems extreme, and carries with it the potential for turning a contained nuisance into a building-wide disaster. A call to the plumber and a sign on the bathroom door saying "sink out of order" might be the better route to take.

There is one last measure you may want to consider. It involves using chemical drain cleaner, but you *must* follow the manufacturer's directions. Read them at least two or three times. Usually they tell you to open it, pour it in, and wait awhile (not like the one-minute miracles on the television, we're talking hours). And because the chemical is so strong, once you have committed to trying it, you can't go back to the physical (plunger/coat hanger) approach. So go ahead, pour it in and wait. This is the time to pull out a good book or several magazines you've been saving for a day at the beach. Writing letters at this stage may cause some alarm to your correspondent, ignorant of why your tone comes from the very depths. Whatever you decide to do while you wait, consider setting a timer so that you don't forget the work in progress.

Retrieving the errant heirloom

Now, for the reader who watched with horror as the borrowed treasure disappeared down the drain—take heart, you may actually be able to retrieve it. With luck, the water was not running at the time of the accident, and you have not for some insane reason allowed the water to begin running since that time. Look underneath the sink and become familiar with the construction of the pipes by comparing them to the diagram. There will probably be some residual water in the trap, and you might want to put a bucket (kitchen bowl, wastepaper basket, empty milk carton) underneath to keep the residue from spilling onto the floor. Get out your handy-dandy adjustable wrench. If you are lucky, there will be a

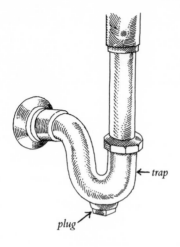

small plug on the underside of the lowest part of the trap. Simply unscrew the plug, allow the trap to drain, and fish around inside the trap (if you have to) to find the missing treasure. If there is no plug, you will have to remove the entire trap.

Anytime you are disassembling a whole into its many parts, do what you can to remember what it looked like when it was working (make a rough sketch, put the parts on the floor in the order they connected, use your Polaroid). Unscrew the two rings with the adjustable wrench. Tip the lower end into the bucket, dumping its contents before your anxious eyes. If the treasure isn't there, and you are sure the trap is clean, you are in bigger trouble than you thought. Don't turn on or flush any water. Call the plumber and be willing to pay the emergency rates (it will ultimately be cheaper than replacing the heirloom). While you are waiting, you might begin composing a letter explaining just how this unfortunate event happened, how sorry you are, and what you would like to do in terms of repayment. Facing this kind of situation squarely will always be better than a lifetime of prayers for early senility. And, if the plumber comes back with the goods, you will be twice rewarded. First, as you gratefully receive the coated, almost unrecognizable item, and then again, as you watch the ammonia and water solution you have prepared (using a ratio of 1:1) in a small bowl (not the sink, please) eat away at the nasty whatever it is, while you tear up the letter of one million apologies and swear that you will never again borrow such a priceless item.

HOW TO
SEW ON A BUTTON

❖

The drama of the absent button: Fathers curse the local laundry service, "They don't call it a mangle iron for nothing." Roommates confess, "But I need to borrow your magenta silk blouse because mine's lost a button and you know magenta's the only color that works with this suit." It can also be somewhat embarrassing. (One earthshaking sneeze that brought your skirt down around your knees.) You pretend no one notices when you're missing a button; you know it's a lie. The unkempt look risks becoming permanent because you haven't the ability to remedy the situation.

It's really very easy to sew on a button (don't be fooled by the length of these directions, just look at the pictures), and it will save you a world of time.

First, make every effort to retrieve the button (with the exception of those in more than one piece). Matching buttons is a time-consuming project, which means that you may have to retire the garment temporarily while you shop (because it is now missing two buttons, the one you lost and the one you need to carry with you at all times on the off chance that you will find yourself inside a button shop). Size, color, number of holes—all are critical to a perfect match, and at the same time don't deserve the memory space required. So, save the button. Take it home, turn on a good, strong light, take out a needle, and choose a thread to match the color of the thread used on the other buttons.

Pull approximately eighteen inches of thread from the spool and clip it off with a pair of scissors. In your haste, you may be tempted to use your front teeth. The only problem with this otherwise efficient move is that the thread tends to come untwisted. An untwisted thread may have two or three "heads" to coordinate through the eye of the needle, as opposed to a twisted thread that presents a single point. After much wetting, twisting, and several unsuccessful efforts to thread the gnawed end, you'll find that the scissored end is preferable.

The actual threading can be done quite easily with steady hands and reasonably good eyesight. Holding the needle between the thumb and forefinger of your left hand, position it to be between the brightest source of light and your eye. Hold the end of the thread between the thumb and forefinger of your right hand, allowing for a lead of perhaps ¼". Steadily guide the thread toward the eye of the needle, through the eye and well out the other side so that it is easy to grab onto. Taking care not to pull the other end through, even up the ends and knot them. You can do this by laying the needle down and making a loop close to the two ends, then pulling the ends up through the backside of the loop. Or you can take the foolproof, if less hygenic, method of licking your thumb and forefinger, taking the ends of the thread, wrapping them around your forefinger, and rubbing your forefinger and thumb back and forth two or three times. Then, pressing the two fingers together (holding the snarled ends), pull the needle and attached thread with your other hand until you feel a knot form at the end of the line.

Should your eyesight or steadiness of hand be below par for this exercise, here is a different approach: Drape the thread over the needle as it is held horizontally. Pull the thread from both ends, making a sharp crease in the thread where it meets the needle. Holding the thread as close to the needle as you can, slip the needle out and thread the crease through the eye. If the crease is sharp enough, the threading should be successful.

There are also those funny tin foil medals, the ones that look like a coin attached to an arrowhead ending in a single wire **V**. They actually work, if you know how to use them. Simply push the diamond-shaped loop of wire all the way through the needle's eye. Put one end of the

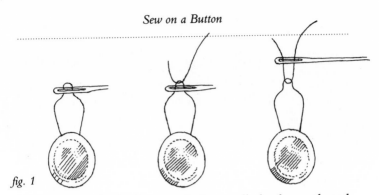

fig. 1

thread through the loop and then pull the loop, thread and all, back through the needle's eye (fig. 1).

Presto! The needle is threaded and it's time to place the button. If you can find the needle holes in the fabric left by the previous button you are in luck. If you have limped along without the button for some time, laundering the garment may have erased those markings and you will need to place the button. Button up the garment (as much as you can). If you are missing the top or bottom button, try to line up the neckband/shirttail by holding the top/bottom firmly in one hand and pulling the bottom/top down with the other. Everything being as straight as possible, you then put a pencil through the buttonhole and make a light mark on the fabric below. That is just where the center of your button should be placed. (On a dark fabric, put the tip of a knife that has been dipped in flour or talc—whichever is more readily available—through the buttonhole.)

Don't sew the button on any old whichway. Look at the method used on the other buttons. Some manufacturers follow the square of a four-hole button, others use the **X**, still others form double vertical lines (fig. 2). Holding the button in place with one hand, take the threaded needle in your free hand, and, underneath the fabric, poke it up and through a hole in the button. Pull

fig. 2

the thread until it is completely through with the exception of the knot (fig. 3). Next, take the needle and put it through the second hole in the button and on out the backside of the fabric (fig. 4). If there are four holes, secure the position of the button by working all four positions (in and out left, in and out right) (fig. 5). The

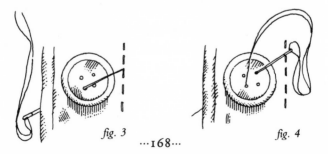

fig. 3   *fig. 4*

thread should make the same pattern on the back of the fabric as you will see on the front of the button. With a double thread, two passes (four threads between holes) should do the trick—a third if you really want to be sure.

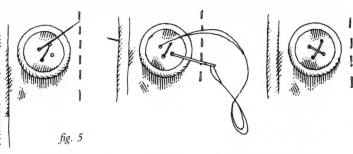

fig. 5

If the button has a metal loop instead of holes, follow the same basic procedure, pulling the thread first through the back of the fabric, then up and through the metal loop and back down again through the fabric. To finish the process, with the needle on the backside of the garment catch up the sewn threads and pull through until you have formed a small loop. Put the needle through the loop and pull to form a knot.

If the fabric is thick (a jacket or coat), and the button is supposed to be functional as opposed to decorative, there should be a space (close to the thickness of the fabric) between the button and the front of the garment. This is easily created by placing a wooden matchstick under the button before you begin to sew. After the button is secure, bring the needle from the back to the front, slide the matchstick out, hold the button away from the fabric and wrap the thread several times around the attaching threads. This binds them together, and keeps them from looking as if the button were about to fall off . . . again.

HOW TO REPAIR A HEM

❖

You *know* you shouldn't pull on a loose thread. You've heard that advice over and over since the beginning of time. And yet, in your haste to look absolutely neat as a pin, you seize that errant thread and before your very eyes the lining drops out of your sleeve, your skirt becomes longer on one side, your cuff is lost in your shoe. You stand there, transformed, from polished to pathetic in one pull.

And, while you are mentally writing on the blackboard fifty lines of "I will never pull on a loose thread again," you decide whether you have time to mend the hem and wear what you had on, or change into something different, saving the mending for later. Of course later comes most often around I-have-nothing-to-wear time. Maybe with these simple instructions you will be inspired to make the repairs right away.

In the preceding chapter, there are instructions about how to thread a needle. You should choose a thread that matches what was used on the previous hem. Today the manufacturer's thread of choice seems to be something resembling fishline, a clear, plastic line. For home repairs, we suggest you use a thread that is as close as possible to the color and weight of the material (you don't want the stitching to show, and a stronger thread tends to tear a lighter fabric). Once the needle has been threaded, put a knot in one end only, leaving the other end free. The free end should always be slightly shorter than the knotted one (take care not to have it be so short that it pulls out every time you take a stitch).

A hem is nothing more than the end of a piece of material that has been turned under. It may have been turned under twice, or it may be bound by a narrow strip of material (seam binding). Either way, the edge of the hem is finished so that your stitching will not pull through an unraveling or "raw" edge. If you find that the hem you are repairing has come apart because the material has done the same, you should create a finished edge by ironing a ¼" fold. Or buy some seam binding and stitch one edge to the raw edge and the other to the back of the skirt.

Catching the underside of the finished/folded edge with your threaded needle, pull the thread through until the knot is fast. Then put the needle through the material at the point directly behind the stitch in the hem (fig. 1), and do your best to incorporate only one or two strands of the garment as you bring the needle back inside (in other words make the tiniest stitch possible, don't put the

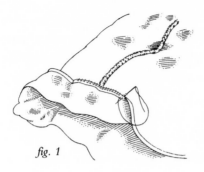

fig. 1

needle in at one point and pull it back through some inches away . . . yes, it would be quicker, but it would also look as if a kindergarten class had collectively done the work . . . and the chances of one of those giant stitches catching on the next chair you sit in are very good indeed.

Think of the stitch as a partial knot. The thread goes around (out and in again) a small section of the outside piece, then through the edge of the hem, then over the stitch just made and ½" along the line to the next stitch (fig. 2). When you have overlapped onto the hem that is

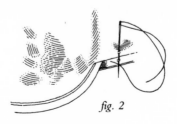

fig. 2

still in place by about an inch, it is time to make several stitches in the same place, pull the needle through forming a loop, guide the needle back through the loop and pull to form a full knot.

Short cuts

If you are in a tremendous hurry, and this really is the only thing you have to wear, there are some shortcuts. They don't stand up to much in the way of wear (that means don't depend on them for any length of time, and definitely not through a washing or dry-cleaning), but in an emergency, you could try:

Safety pins: Little ones can do the trick as long as it isn't the whole hem. Remember the part about picking up only one or two strands of the visible side. Never try this with straight pins . . . ouch!

Iron-on tape: You can find it in your local fabric store. It works with the help of your iron (not too hot). Just follow the instructions and vow to replace it with the real thing on Saturday morning.

Masking tape: It's reported to work, but only for a very short time, so use it if you must but with the same vow pledged when using the iron-on variety.

HOW TO POLISH SHOES

❖

"Beware of all enterprises that require new clothes," warned the guru of antiestablishmentarians, H.D. Thoreau, and generations cheered. What better source of reasoning to ignore the dress code for graduation exercises or Cousin Cecile's wedding? But what of the situation that simply requires a polished appearance . . . the wearing of old clothes made to look like new? We've talked about ironing that handsome, cotton dress shirt. We've mentioned replacing buttons and checking that drooping hemline with a stitch or two. Surely you have a tie from the Christmas before you were bold enough to drop Granny a hint about your cash-flow situation. And there you stand, clean, pressed, mended, right down to your toes, which brings us to the subject at hand. Sneakers won't do. They may be comfortable, funky, the only thing in your closet, but they just won't do. So drag out the pair of leather sturdy browns or modest pumps your mother made you buy for your first college interview and put them on. Sure they're dusty. No, they don't make you look weird, but they do need a little polish.

Dad used to have a wooden box, one that latched shut with a shoe rest for the handle, and inside were cans that read Brown or Black or even Cordovan, whatever that was. There were also brushes, one was small with a handle and stiff bristles, "It's for getting the polish out of the tin and putting it on the shoe . . . you don't need to use so much!" The other had a rectangular back with softer bristles, "It's what you use to shine the shoe." And there was a strip of heavy flannel cloth, which may have been replaced by a diaper or a garish argyle, smudged with brown, black, and cordovan. "You use it to spread the polish around and work it into the leather." This talent, if learned at an early age, took a lot of practice and some serious thought. "Do I put polish on the stitching? What about the heel? Does it matter if polish gets on the edge of the sole, or if I slip and it does get on just a little bit, should I make it look like I meant to do that by putting it all the way around? Will black polish wash out of a white sock?" You probably lack the time and eager curiosity you had when you were five and are only hoping for direct steps, one through eight. Well, here they are.

Take the shoes off. In the airport, professional shoeshiners will never ask you to, but keep in mind they do this for a living, you are doing it for the first time. You take the shoes off because polish does not wash out of socks or stockings. Should the day come when shoe polishing is an integral part of your morning routine, you may put your foot up on the bedrail perilously near the eyelet dust ruffle with the confidence of a tightrope walker. Today, you should be content to lay out a piece of yesterday's newspaper and let your hand replace the foot to steady the shoe.

The more formal the shoe, the farther it has been from the front of the closet, allowing plenty of time to collect feathers, dog hairs, dust kitties, not to mention sand and dirt from other shoes that routinely land on top of the poor forgotten souls. First step is to "dry" clean the shoe. If you last wore this magnificent pair at Randy's wedding in Virginia (remember how hard it rained, and how red that clay was?) you may need to use a brush to remove the dirt lodged between the heel and the sole. Otherwise, just a quick rub against your pant leg should do the trick. (You are wearing old clothes, aren't you?)

Unless you are the one in a thousand who believes that no purchase of shoes is complete without the matching polish, your personal collection of polish may be small to nonexistent. The grocer may carry an impressive array of polish, some of it in bottles, some in jars, and some in tins. Your selection should be based upon color and material. Leather is polished with wax (the crayonlike substance found in a tin or the more colorful varieties of a whipped butter consistency found in the jar). Synthetics are polished with paint (spray on, sponge-on liquids found in bottles). A word about the bottled variety of "polish" and why it is best left for synthetic materials. What was once a living, breathing cow's hide, is now your leather shoe. A waxy polish not only brings a shine, it restores the dried, tired hide. Think of it as a skin product designed to carry on where Ponce de Leon left off. On the other hand, a liquid paint, posing as a thirty-second miracle, will ultimately speed the aging process. Think of it as "pancake" makeup, perfect for the bright lights of the moment, but oh, what it does to the real you. (White shoes leave little option. Saddle soap and clear wax are honorable, but liquid white polish wins the "Whitest Award.") While these leather shoes may be far from your favorites, it is reasonable to assume that they may be called into duty as often as you are. Keeping them young and beautiful is to your mutual advantage. They'll last a lifetime, and you'll go up a notch or two on the confidence scale just knowing that your formal garb is ready when you are.

Let's get on with the procedure. A daub of wax polish, applied either with the stiff bristle brush ("dauber") or a corner of the cloth, is spread evenly, but not heavily, over the top, sides, and back of the shoe. If you drive to work, if you drive at all, the back of your shoes are taking a beating—evident only to those who stand behind you in an interminable line at the bank, sit behind you at the outdoor wedding, kneel behind you during the funeral. Rather like a wad of gum stuck in the back of your hair, scuffed heels are a sign of a half-hearted try. So, the polish is on the shoe and gently worked into the leather, covering scuffs and masking scratches, with the dauber or cloth. In the interest of efficiency, you may as well polish the other shoe before you begin to shine the shoes.

As with any task, the proper equipment facilitates the chore. In this case, a few strokes with a soft bristle brush will give you a quick and easy shine. Put your left hand in the shoe, and the shoe on the paper. Holding the brush in your right hand, use a right–left, right–left across the top, and a series of right–lefts around the sides and back and the job is done. No brush? No problem, really. Take the soft cloth in both hands, leaving a ten-inch span of cloth in between, and put the shoe on your bare foot. Using a back and forth motion, pull the cloth repeatedly over the shoe's surfaces. It's slightly more work, but you will achieve the same effect. The pros use a combination of the two methods: First the brush for a preliminary shine, and then, with just a little more polish (and, some will tell you, a slight misting of water), the cloth for a final buffing.

A quick check to make sure there are no clumps of unburnished polish just waiting to rub onto your hem. If you're planning to wear these shoes at the rehearsal dinner three nights from tonight, but you need to pack them now, we suggest a plastic bag and shoe trees, real or substitutes (see chapter on how to pack a bag). No reason to look as if you came through with the baggage.

You may have given yourself an afternoon for this exercise, and found, to your surprise and delight, that it actually took less time to polish the shoes than it did to read the chapter. This being the case, why not look through the closet and see if you have any other leather shoes or boots that might benefit from a little attention.

HOW TO GIVE
A TRIM

❖

Politically, culturally, historically, we pay a great deal of attention to hair. The subject of song and verse, fable and fact, tresses and their significance form an unbroken strand throughout the ages. Whether it is conditioning or genes, few are able to respond with indifference to the desperate friend's, "What am I going to do about my hair?" It may be twelve midnight, or the Sunday afternoon before the most important interview of his or her career, but it's clearly too late to quell the lamentations with a call to Delila's in hopes of a last-minute cancellation. The only consolation may be to offer a personal touch: "I could give you a little trim if you like."

Given the value placed on physical appearances, and the disproportionate importance given to one's hair, this kind offer may be immediately refused on the reasonable grounds that you lack professional training, the theory being that the "windblown" look is preferable to one better described as "molting." However, if you truly believe that your friend's future could only be enhanced by even the most feeble attempt to neaten the nob, you can begin to allay the fears by repeating the following patter. "You really should start taking some time for yourself. What do you think, I close my eyes at the hairdresser's? I've seen it done a million times. It won't take a minute, just relax. How do you live with that schedule anyway, so demanding, do this do that, rush, rush, rush, and oh, by the way, be gorgeous? Really, close your eyes and try to relax."

The equipment

You don't need much equipment. What you do need has to be the right kind. The sharpest scissors you can find are essential. If you can only find a pair that has been used for cutting paper or wire, ask for a knife sharpener (see chapter on carving a turkey). Dull scissors give more of a bend and pull to the hair, slowing the process and decreasing the overall comfort level for everyone involved. A comb, a towel, and a razor (for the finishing touches) should be easy enough to come by. Wet hair is easier to cut, and a straight-back chair encourages appropriate posture. If possible, try to seat your subject in front of a mirror. The cut will become a joint effort ("What do you think, a little more off the sides?") and the responsibility for the results can be shared.

The technique

Begin with reassuring phrases like, "I'm not going to cut very much, this is just a trim." (Drape the towel around her neck, she'll be happy to hold it in place.) "I'm following the cut you had before, okay? (Comb out the tangles.) "We'll just take care of the split ends."

Analyze the cut: Was it layered or was it meant to be all one length? Was it very short in the back or should there be enough to gently turn under? Engage your friend in this analysis, asking for her interpretation of how it once looked. Having established a fair idea of what you are hoping to recapture, find the part. You can use the consultant's approach . . . "On which side do you usually part your hair?" or, if the subject's eyes have taken on that passive, faraway look, resort to the pioneer technique . . . find it yourself by evenly combing the hair on top of the head straight back and then gently pushing it forward until a clean, narrow avenue presents itself. At first glance, there may seem to be several avenues to choose from. Take the one that begins farthest back on the head. Cowlicks, a colloquialism for unruly swirls acquired at birth, often serve as the starting point for a part. (Cowlicks along the forehead have been addressed by the previous barber, and you can gratefully follow his lead.) Now, begin to think of the hair in sections. Top left of the part, top right of the part, left side, back, and right side. Remember, this is only a trim. You are simply trying to even the ends and neaten the appearance. Resist the urge to make a drastic change, and never cut more than ¼" at a time. Start with the back of the head, for no other reason than to give yourself a safe practice zone. (This advice should not be shared. Think of it as a wink from the author. Once you have gained some confidence you will be ready to work under the steady gaze of your friend.)

For a layered cut: Gently hold up a section of hair, running from the top of the back to the middle of the back about ½" wide, straight out from the head using your index and middle fingers. Continue sliding your fingers out, away from the head, until they hold the last ½" from the ends. Following the somewhat jagged line formed by the tired, split ends, cut ¼" to make healthy, even ends. Let the strands drop, and take up the next section. Holding the hair straight out at a 90° angle and making only a ¼" cut guarantees that the trim will be uniform. Continue using this method for the lower half of the back, and then start in on the sides. Remember, these sections are vertical—trimming on the horizontal will result in well-defined bands, as if your friend has been wearing three or four different hats for the past two days.

Finish with the top, holding it straight up in sections that run from ear to ear. If the cut is long and layered, have your friend bend her head over, comb the hair down over her face and simply even the ends. If the cut is supposed to be all one length, part the hair evenly from the crown of the head to the back of the neck and bring the two sections around to the front, as if you were going to make pigtails. Trim straight across.

For the finishing touches, be sure to take care of neck and sideburn hairs that may also have outgrown the original style. The shorter the haircut, the more important these details become. Here's where the mirror will be most helpful. "Do you want me to leave those curls that stick out behind your ears? What vintage are your sideburns?" Don't clip or shave beyond (underneath) the natural hairline or you will create a sidewall effect that will take weeks to grow out. Work slowly, be gentle, and try to avoid any sharp intake of breath, or expressions of dismay. "Whoops. Uh, oh." You don't want a sudden turn of the head to interrupt your work or to necessitate another round of trimming just to even things up with that last chop. (Again, in the interest of reducing nervous twitching, keep the styptic pencil hidden in your pocket.) When you think you have finished, remove the towel, do what you can to brush away cuttings that may have fallen between the towel and neck (using a blow dryer or a dry towel), and tell your friend how fantastic she looks. Like a million dollars.

The result

Surprise tempered with relief for the cuttee. Self-esteem elevated by relief for the cutter. A few rules to follow, however: The now presentable friend must promise to make and keep an appointment with a professional hairdresser of choice within the next two weeks. Observation of this rule will preclude a repeat performance, which has a very good chance of turning out less evenly. After all, the first trim was based on a professional cut, any subsequent snips would be following novice, albeit well-intentioned, lines. Because the emergency treatment was so successful, it might be assumed that there was some potential for moonlighting. The cuttee finds the price to be just right, the cutter is thrilled with tangible evidence of unsuspected talent, and before six months have run, the relationship once bolstered by tonsorial dependency will be strained by social demands to "get a real haircut, why don'tcha?"

Coda: Perhaps your friend turns out to be the same one mentioned on every radio talk show . . . "I have a friend who wanted me to ask about the accuracy of do-it-yourself pregnancy tests . . ." and everyone knows who that friend is. What if you are the one who has cancelled out of five appointments at the hairdresser's, and you are the one who is convinced that your hair alone will torpedo tomorrow's interview, and you are interested in giving not just anyone, but yourself, a trim. At this point it is a good idea to take an objective step backward and determine your current level of desperation. If it is somewhere between dashing/screaming and kicking/sobbing, you should not be operating a pair of sharp scissors. Why not try some mousse and a couple of high-fashion combs? Or hairspray—the product *is* new and improved. Your head no longer looks as if it has been dipped in a vat of polyurethane (it's only when you stand outside in a gale-force wind that anyone will guess you've been maintaining your coiffure with Mannequin Mist). A jaunty chapeau or a sixties-style bandanna may work for the cab ride, but wearing hats indoors indefinitely is a debatable move. The more positive approach would be to give yourself a good shampoo, some conditioner, a gentle comb-out, a little help from the dryer, all the while thinking about how you would run the meeting if it were yours to run.

HOW TO
BACK UP A TRAILER

❖

All the experts agree: don't back up a trailer if you can possibly avoid it. The next time you see a gentleman in a baseball cap, T-shirt and mirrored sunglasses, ten feet above your head, corkscrewed three-quarters in his seat and halfway out the window of the cab, backing his rig off a distractingly congested two-way street into a remarkably narrow space, stop and take off your own cap. What he's doing is no mean feat and it deserves your admiration and respect. Nevertheless, avoid it if you can.

Willingness to lend a hand, a hopeful outlook on life, a belief that if everybody hung back nothing would ever get done—all of these are wonderful virtues. Still, before you volunteer to back up your new roommate's U-Haul or the boat trailer or, God forbid, the horse trailer, think twice. Isn't there something else you'd be better at? Or someone who'd be better at this task than you? There's nobody else, and you'll have to pay another day's rent if you don't return the trailer, unloaded, by 5:00 P.M.? Well then, go ahead and read the directions below.

It's a good idea to start with the overall concept, sort of like the game of charades. Look around for something in the apartment or nearby neighborhood that is small and has two sets of parallel wheels. Your mother's luggage has little wheels, doesn't it? What about your neighbor's stroller or that old pair of roller skates? Whatever you find, think of it as the trailer. Think of your body as the car. Put your left hand under your right elbow, and your right elbow over your belly button. The hand cupping the elbow will act as the pivot point (think of the ball on your car's rear bumper) and the forearm will serve as the tongue of the trailer. Hold onto the wheeled apparatus (or imagine you are holding onto one) with your right hand. As you move the "trailer" to the left, you will see that your body must turn to the right. The converse is true (even if your elbow won't allow you to prove it). Confused? How much time do you have? If there is no trailer backing in your immediate future, now is a good time to get out some 3" × 5" index cards and Scotch tape. Cut a ½" × 3" strip off of one card and tape it to the same card midway along the 3" side, so that it forms a right angle and the two together look like a simplified trailer without wheels. Poke a hole in the free end of the "tongue." (Use a straight pin, safety pin, pen point, whatever is handy.) Poke a hole in the second card ("My Alfa" reads the vanity plate) midway along the 3" side, ¼" from the edge. If you are in someone's office supply closet, look around for a brad (those brass colored things that look like a mushroom head with legs). Chances are you aren't in such a closet, so you'll have to come up with a makeshift pivot—a straight pin, thumbtack, straightened staple—you'll come up with something. There you have a model car, attached to a model trailer. All you need is some privacy and time to play, moving it around, backing and filling around the chair leg, between the sofa and coffee table. Remember, you can only push with the front of the car. Keep any of this that proved to be helpful in mind as you climb in behind the wheel of the car.

Would it be possible to practice for a while in an open lot? Isn't there a school nearby? Or a shopping center? (They are usually well-lit and not too busy after 9:00 P.M.) You can practice with a loaded trailer as easily as you can with an empty one. And just like everything else, practice is what you need. That guy you watched backing up the eighteen wheeler didn't do it on the first try, you know. He spent the better part of six months in a driving school parking lot working on these moves. The only difference between him and you is a willingness to practice. So go to it.

Begin by aligning the trailer with the car so that as you put the car in reverse and back up, both are in a straight line. The next series of steps should be done as SLOWLY as possible, really, just one rpm above stalling or bucking. To turn the trailer to the LEFT, turn the wheel of the car as tightly as you can to the RIGHT, never taking your eyes off the left wheel of the trailer. Slowly, slowly, continue backing until the wheel of the trailer has reached the angle you need to negotiate the driveway (or imagined alley). What do we mean? The angle you need? Well, look at the wheel of the trailer, and simply project a straight line from that wheel. Does the line cross over the flower bed and up to the front porch? Does it run straight into the brick wall? Or does it lead neatly up the barn ramp? The third angle is the one you need. And as soon as that angle is achieved, stop and crank the wheel of the car (while you are stopped) all the way around to the LEFT. Slowly, SLOWLY continue backing until your car is once again aligned with the trailer. This may take some correcting, by moving forward to the left and backward to the right. The trailer will maintain the original angle during all this back and forth action, you are just moving the position—away from or closer to the destination—jockeying your car into alignment with the angled trailer. Once you have made this new alignment, you should be all set—just back her on up, keeping the steering wheel straight. If

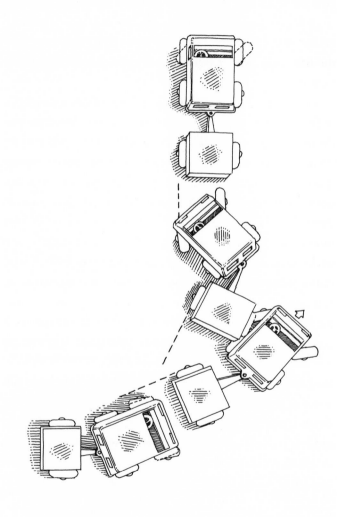

you aren't all set, it may be time to reset the original angle by turning the car wheel in the opposite direction of the way you want the trailer to turn (just like you did the first time. Trailer still needs to go to the LEFT? Then turn the car wheel to the RIGHT).

This all sounds so backward, so counterintuitive, and it feels about the same, at least at first. But read it through again, and keep practicing. It works. Of course there is always the possibility that you don't have time or space to practice, or that you won't have more than an hour's worth of patience to devote to this exercise. Aren't there any shortcuts? Well, of course there are. Number one: never, ever drive into a spot that you can't drive out of (not back out of, drive out of), even if it means pulling into the "trucks only" section of the thruway's rest area. Double-parking while you unload works in the more friendly neighborhoods, and once you've unloaded you can keep on driving straight up to the doorway of the Rental Headquarters. Did you volunteer to take a load of brush to the dump only to discover that neither you nor your friend can remember how to turn a trailer around, and the dumpmeister is on a late lunch break? If the trailer isn't too heavy, and you have already emptied the load, you might consider unhitching the trailer (be careful, even light trailers are heavy). Before you do, look around for a log or a big rock, anything that is as tall as the hitch ball is on your car. Put the log under the tongue and unhitch the trailer. (This little trick prevents you from throwing your back out as you try to lift the tongue up off the ground). Drive the car around so that it is facing in the direction of the exit arrow, and back it up to within a tongue-and-a-half's length of the unhitched trailer. With the help of your friend, pick up the tongue and carry the trailer around to meet the rear of the car. Bring the supporting log or rock along if you can. Hitching the trailer back up will be much easier if the tongue is resting only two or three inches below ball level, particularly if you have to let go of the tongue and get back into the car to inch it—just a tiny bit—toward the trailer. This is when your friend had better have a good set of lungs and you need to keep your eyes on all three rear view mirrors at once. "Hold it, that's far enough," is just what you are waiting to hear. Screw the cup onto the ball, secure the safety chain, and don't forget those little wires that have to be reconnected—otherwise your brake and turn signal lights won't be of much use and after all that work you won't be in any mood to humor the officer in blue.

HOW TO GO SAILING

❖

The next time you overhear someone gush, "Gee, I've always wanted to go horseback riding," position yourself to observe the equestrienne's reaction. Do you think her sudden silence signifies *disdain*? Or, should you be standing in a long line at the Dairy Queen when your younger sister turns to the tattooed trucker behind her and squeals, "It must be neat to drive one of those big rigs across the country," ask yourself, does he roll his eyes at you in disbelief? Could be. Whether it is disdain or disbelief, the reaction generally means, "Not with me you don't!" Isn't it strange the unintended effect innocent enthusiasm has on the ego of a professional?

The exception to that stiff arm's length seems to come whenever we hear, "You know, I've never been sailing." Invariably, an invitation to end that unthinkable deprivation by climbing aboard the commodore's sloop is just around the buoy. So, if you find yourself being drawn to the stories and pictures that surround your host's yacht club trophies, and your exuberance leads to such an invitation, go ahead, accept with pleasure, but be prepared.

Sailing is rarely a passive experience. Even the greenest guest has a responsibility to make the outing as smooth as possible. Your dinner host, so genial, so solicitous while carving the roast the night before, may appear to have suffered a personality change as he checks the rigging next morning. Names like Queeg and Bligh surface alongside Jekyll and Hyde. It must be something in the water. You'll find that a seasoned crew behave much like members of a dysfunctional family. Steeled against the blustering, keeping their heads down, ears open, never willing to take the initiative but always ready to react, these hearty mates will make light of the tension and encourage you to enjoy the voyage. If your carefree childhood was spent at the Commune of Peace and Love where you never once heard a voice raised in anger, if your sensitive nature is easily cowed by authoritarians wearing nautical caps, this chapter is for you.

Travel books always recommend that you learn a few polite phrases of the national language when traveling in a foreign country. Nautical terminology isn't an entirely foreign language—the syntax is English—but it might as well be. Though fluency is not required, it's often assumed during emergencies, real or imagined. So, in addition to reading the short list below, you may want to make yourself a set of flash cards and test yourself repeatedly. Flash cards develop memory and hand-eye coordination, both of which are at a premium when under sail.

Captain (skipper): Most often your host, clearly the boss. Watchwords are: "Listen and Obey." When he appears to be relaxed, you may ask the captain for instruction. When he is working, keep your questions to yourself and do what you are told to do—the quicker the better. (For more on questions, see page 202.)

Line: A rope (they come in a variety of diameters). "That line" is the rope nearest you. "Grab that line" means take hold of the wildly flapping rope nearest you, or release the taut one from whatever is holding it—look at the "line" and make it do what it isn't doing.

Sheet: A rope that is attached to the corner of the sail, used to regulate the amount of wind filling the sail.

Painter: A rope that is attached to the bow of the boat, used to fasten the boat to the mooring or dock.

Cleats: In this case have nothing to do with footwear. Mounted on the rail (gunnel) of the boat, these metal arms extend beyond their wooden base to help secure the lines. There is an appropriate technique for wrapping the rope, but in an emergency cleats can be used once-around, just to spare your hand from rope burn. Don't see any cleats? There may be what looks like a pair of gears in place of the cleat—a jam cleat by name, because you actually jam the rope between the gears. You probably won't be asked to use the cleats unless you have asked for and been given some instruction.

Dingy (tender): The small boat, propelled either by rowing oars or a small motor. This little boat waits at the dock to take you to the sailboat. You may not need to know how to row or start the motor, but you do need to remember that all small boats are tippy. Keep your weight low and sit where you are told to sit (the skipper is tactfully trying to balance the load without having to ask how much each passenger weighs).

Bow: (pronounced as in "bow wow") The front, and most often the pointy end, of the boat.

Stern: The rear, and most often the flat end, of the boat.

Port: The left side of the boat (when you are facing the bow); easy to remember, four letters in p-o-r-t; four letters in l-e-f-t.

Starboard: The right side of the boat (facing the bow).

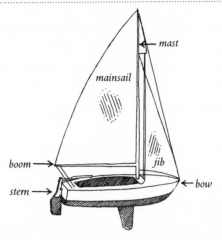

Mast: Tall, upright pole. The sail is "hoisted" up the mast.

Boom: The long, horizontal pole that holds the sail down. When you board the craft, look to see what the clearance is between the head of a seated passenger and the boom. Keep that calculation in mind at all times, but particularly when you hear . . .

"Ready about": This means that the captain is about to change the position of the sail, which will necessitate a complete shift of the boom. His tone of voice will clearly indicate the time alotted to this shift—it's never long. Be ready to duck and move to the opposite side of the boat.

Mooring: Floating marker somewhere in the harbor that is anchored most often by a very large rock or block of cement. The boat is tied to the mooring with the painter (see above). ("Mooring" can also refer to the process of tying up to the buoy or marker.)

The lingo is important, and some review will help you to enjoy your first outing (and a true mastery may be rewarded with additional invitations). As in all cases, however, the lingo is secondary to the basic rules:

What to do: Have a great time, that's why you were invited. At the same time, keep in mind that you are responsible to the captain and for yourself. On a large vessel, you will most probably be invited to stretch out on the deck and enjoy the sail. On a smaller craft you may be told to grab that line.

What to wear: White, soft-soled shoes (don't want to make nasty, black scuff marks on that gleaming white deck, do you?); layers of clothing (number of layers is directly proportional to the distance from the Equator); visored hat; sunglasses (preferably of the polaroid UV filter variety); a small, soft, stowable bag carrying a change of socks, sunblock, and towel.

Use common sense: Queasy on an airplane? Never read in the car? Do everyone a favor and take some Dramamine before you set out for the marina. Wear a life jacket; if the boat tips over—and it probably won't—you can tread water effortlessly while listening for directives. Don't untie the boat until you are asked—many is the outboard motor that refused to start up on a boat that has been prematurely released. For some captains, control freaks in particular, any sort of gaffe brings out the worst. Sharp words, quick, almost desperate movements, rushing about holding one line in his teeth, winching in a second, steadying the tiller with his knee . . . a word to the wise . . . as comical as this scene may appear, gales of laughter are best kept for the car ride home—provided you depart in separate cars.

Use common courtesy: Be willing to help. Your ability has more to do with the size of the craft than your actual experience or physical strength. The smaller the boat, the more capable you will appear to be (from mere passenger to seadog—it's all in the eyes of the beholder, in this case, the captain). So do state quickly and clearly, if you did not, that you did not understand a command. If you are in the bow and coming to shore, don't jump off the boat empty-handed—take the painter with you and offer to secure the boat ("Do you want a double hitch or bowline? Or shall I just hold onto it?") Failure to take advantage of this initial ship-to-shore contact may result in a completely unintended second sail of the day for the crew and captain whom you unwittingly have set adrift.

Use nautical etiquette: If the Commodore or Vice Commodore of the yacht club is expected on board, treat him like royalty (everyone else does). For most of us, this eventuality is as likely as dining with the Queen. In either instance, attentive if not downright deferential behavior is not only appropriate but expected. Follow your host's lead (literally, onto and off of the vessel). The exception might be a salute exchanged between the commanding officer and the crew (think of this as a secret society's handshake—it's not something for an outsider to fake).

Be careful: Do not put your hands on the gunnels (railings) when you are boat-to-boat or boat-to-pier. When it is time to disembark and you move toward the side of the boat, it begins to tip with your weight and you naturally want to grab onto the side for balance if nothing else—but don't, because . . . ieee, yieee, yiii! . . . the space between the boat and the dock or dinghy can vary from twenty-plus to zero inches in a flash, with alarming force and absolutely no regard for bone or flesh between.

Ask questions: Two questions in particular, should be asked while you are standing on the dock: "Did Alison tell you, I never learned how to swim?" If you don't know how, and you are brave enough to get into a boat anyway, you must be bold enough to alert your host to this gap in your education. Blame it on your parents, growing up in the desert or along the Maine coast—just be sure to mention it. The other question has to do with the amount of coffee you consumed before climbing aboard. "Tell me, are there any secrets to operating the head?" has an objective, amused-with-the-human-condition tone to it. Other guests, particularly those given to bluffing, will silently applaud your leadership and the captain, who has "head tales" that would curl your hair, will lead the ovation.

Knots

In this instance, a few pictures are worth at least a few thousand words. We'll start by defying that wisdom in a verbal description of how to tie a bowline and two half-hitches. If you begin to feel like a four-year-old at the feet of Houdini, take a look at the diagrams. There's nothing magic about tying knots. The bowline is most often used when you are tying a boat to a mooring (another rope with a loop at the end). The two half-hitches are more popular for tying up at the dock (around a post or upright). Once again, practice makes perfect, so drag out a shoelace, or piece of twine or rope if you have any, and give it a try.

To tie a bowline: Gauge the length of rope needed to make a sizeable loop and add another foot to use in making the knot (say the total is two feet). So, holding the rope in your left hand two feet from its end, and in your right hand eighteen inches from the end, bring your right hand up and onto the top of your left hand, forming a loop in the rope (fig. 1). Hold the loop with your left hand and bring the tail down, around and up through the loop (coming from behind) (fig. 2). Continue to hold the first loop with your left hand and bring the tail farther up and around the rope just above your left hand and then take it down through the loop your left hand is still holding (fig. 3). That's a bowline. Follow the diagram, it's much easier.

To tie a clove-hitch: You have one success with knots, why not go for two? To tie up a boat with two half-hitches, sometimes called a clove hitch and looks like the letter Z: Take the loose end of the rope and go around the post. Cross over the top of the rope, forming a half-hitch, and go down and around the post a second time, forming a diagonal line. Bring the end back around and put it between the bottom of the diagonal and the post, forming another half-hitch. Then out the other side. Slip the first half-hitch down to meet the second half-hitch,

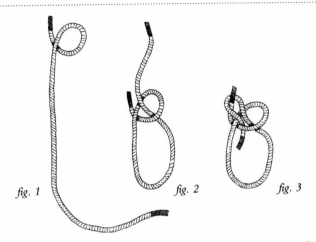

fig. 1   fig. 2   fig. 3

to make two half-hitches (fig. 4). Pull tight. Again, the diagram says it all.

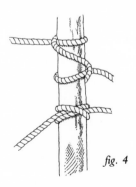

fig. 4

What the diagrams don't say, but you might imply with, "I'd feel better if someone would check my knots," is that while you've done your best, the responsibility for the boat rests with the skipper and your pride will not go before a drifting dinghy.

HOW TO ENTERTAIN
A PARTY OF SIX

❖

This chapter is written for the person who is neither terrified nor bored by its title. If the reader's reaction is, "Six people for dinner, oh my gawd!" all the reassurances in the world will do that reader no good. Best to take your friends to a restaurant you can afford or send them a nice fruitcake over the holidays. If, on the other hand, the reader's incredulous reaction is, "Only six! You call that a party?" such a reader will find the following pages dull in the extreme and would be bored in the company they're meant to entertain.

The number six has no special significance. It's a good number to cook for and it allows for general conversation around a table. If your place isn't so small that you sleep standing up, you can probably accommodate six people one way or another. Even if you don't have a table, six people can eat their dinner on their laps, sitting on couches or the floor. Six is small enough that it doesn't feel like an army bivouacked all over your apartment and you won't have to raise your voice to be heard.

Compose your gathering as you like but give some thought to who likes whom, who would provide a good foil for which other guest. A bad idea is to invite the same people you see every day at work; a good idea is to combine friends and acquaintances from different parts of your life. Just as you don't want to serve all white food, or all soft food, or all curried food, you want some variety around the table as well as on it. It makes life more interesting. So do fistfights—perhaps the new and somewhat preachy vegetarian shouldn't be invited to the same dinner as your friends who raise sheep for the wool *and* the meat.

With these precepts out of the way, how do you plan a dinner for six? If you haven't done much entertaining, try to plan in your head—or, better, on paper—what needs to be done ahead of time. Having five friends over for dinner isn't particularly hard but it's a little more complicated than multiplying what you cook for yourself by six and serving it up. For starters, when dining alone, you may not much care how your surroundings look. But you certainly don't want your guests tripping over stacks of magazines or seeing the sad state your houseplants are in. So plan to clean house and figure out when you're going to do it. If you have roommates, they should be invited or tactfully uninvited. An invited roommate might be willing to help out, at least with cleaning his or her room and keeping the common rooms—bathroom, living room, kitchen—at their pristine best.

Plan your menu—let's say there will be a first course, a main course, and some kind of dessert—so that no laws of physics or thermodynamics will have to be violated. Presumably you have only one oven. Therefore you cannot be baking a pie at 350° at the same time you are baking potatoes at 425°. Similarly, if you want to serve hot asparagus and hot pasta, you can't be using the same pot for both five minutes before you intend to bring them to the table. Put another way, while thinking what to serve, think also of how you're going to cook the different dishes and in what sequence. All at the same time in the hour before your guests arrive? Bad idea, unless you have nerves of steel, no common sense and a high degree of eye-hand coordination. Necessity is the mother of invention and the constraints imposed by cooking utensils, cooking services, time, and energy all give you a wonderful opportunity to make a virtue of necessity.

Once you've decided what you're going to serve your friends—and we'll get back to this in a bit—think about how you're going to serve it. How many will you be? Six? Do you have six dinner plates, six wineglasses—or six matching jelly jars—six knives, forks, and spoons? In short, do you have enough of everything or do you need to borrow or buy some stuff? Original as it would be, you don't really want them drinking their aperitifs out of banged-up old Sierra Club cups. They can do that at home. American culture often equates informality with sincerity, the idea being that if you say, "Sit anywhere you like; make yourself at home," and serve your guests on chipped plates and mismatched glasses and napkins, this is somehow a more genuine expression of friendship. Less pretentious. More honest. "Relax," you tell your guests, "I haven't gone to any special trouble." This is okay to say only when it isn't true. Think about it: What's so special about treating your friends no better and possibly worse than they treat themselves? The table doesn't have to be set with Baccarat and Limoges, but do what you can to make it special.

Are you going to serve the plates in the kitchen and bring them to the table or do you have the kind of kitchen in which people will naturally congregate? Will they be there making unhelpful comments and hunting for ice while you're trying to lever the chicken from the bottom of its pan and wondering how lumpy is too lumpy in the mashed potato department? If so, plan on transferring the hot or prepared-ahead-of-time food into serving dishes, arranging them on the counter, plates at one end, and calling it a buffet. Invite your guests to serve themselves. Or, if you have a biggish table and the kind of food you're serving lends itself to this, you can bring the various dishes to the table and hand them around. This makes sense if the food is both good looking and manageable. Sliced tomatoes on a green plate, green beans in a blue bowl, pratically anything on an oval platter, even slices of homely meatloaf—all of these dress up a table.

How to Set the Table

Take advantage of falling standards. There was a time when the absence of finger bowls provoked naughty, conspiratorial laughter from guests. They knew themselves to be in a truly bohemian household, one step up from an opium den. Nowadays, set a table with cloth napkins and candles and the befuddled or callow will ask what the occasion is, while other guests will grow nostalgically maudlin. Your napkins may not be damask, the candles may be stuck in the bottom of custard cups, it's the allusion that counts. Don't be surprised to hear yourself compared to someone's beloved grandmother. And brace yourself for rueful reflections on things not being what they used to be.

There is a correct way to set a table: Napkin to the left of the dinner plate, with fork on or between napkin and plate. To the right of the plate comes the knife, blade turned in, and then the spoon. Are you serving more than one course? Do you have more than one fork and spoon for each guest? If so, you can set the salad fork to the left of the dinner fork and the soup spoon to the right of the teaspoon. Only, of course, if soup is on the menu. This is not meant as a ritual display of silver you inherited from your great aunt or plates you collected from a dozen boxes of laundry detergent.

If you have a bread-and-butter plate, it goes to the left of the fork and napkin. Water and wineglasses go at the tip of the knife. Should your cutlery be so extensive that it includes dessert spoon and fork or should you be serving salad after, rather than before or with the main course, such utensils should go above the dinner plate, parallel to the edge of the table, and, if there are fork and spoon, heading in opposite directions.

Flowers as a centerpiece will mark your dinner as an occasion, even if you're serving something as basic as good pasta, good bread, and a good salad. Again, the flowers are there for your guests to enjoy but they won't enjoy them if they have to talk over or around them. So see the chapter on how to arrange flowers.

Seating

Diplomatic careers have foundered on bad decisions about who should sit where but with six people you've nothing to worry about. Because couples often go through life welded together at the hip, it might make for a more interesting dynamic not to have the same two people who breakfast together every morning of their mortal lives seated together at dinner as well. Convention likes to have a man seated next to a woman seated next to a man seated next to a woman. But since couples no longer come exclusively in those pairings and since your table may not conform to three of one, three of the other, best to seat people for conversational possibility rather than atavistic allegiance.

The reason it's worth thinking about in advance is that you'll be asked the question, "Is there any place in particular you'd like us to sit?" just as you're draining the pasta or taking the muffins out of their tin and your mind will have a hard time switching gears. You want the talkers and the listeners fairly evenly distributed around the table. You probably don't want the three men who were college roommates absorbed in a tête-à-tête-à-tête at one end of the table. Nor do you want the shy cousin who invited you to dinner when you first moved to town to have only you to talk to throughout the meal, the cocktail hour having pretty much exhausted your news of the family. So say firmly, "Yes, I'd like Marjorie on my right, Fritz on my left, and if Betty would go to the other end of the table, the rest of you can sit where you like."

What to Serve

If you've invited people who can talk—a roomful of contemplatives can be spiritually soothing but the ambience is not ideal for a dinner party—it's to be hoped that they will have something to say to one another. In service of this hope, don't plan a menu so dazzling, so obviously the product of long, hot hours in the kitchen that it clobbers all possibility of conversation.

By a similar token, you don't want the food to be memorably bad. So, unless you're an experienced cook or have recently won the lottery and believe your luck will hold, cook something you know. Better a modest success than a spectacular failure. True, a genuinely vile meal will give your guests something to talk about—to others—as soon as they recover. On the other hand, cooking bad enough to be remembered tends to stop conversation as guests come to terms with what you've put before them. Faces fall as they gingerly push the disaster around on their plates. Unless they weren't particularly hungry to begin with or have unusually cheerful natures, the bloom will fade from your evening.

Eliminate from your menu items sure to cause a ruckus. Tripe, say, or brussels sprout puff. If you know that one guest is allergic to walnuts or that another one doesn't eat red meat, modify your menu to accommodate these preferences. Something new could have entered their dietary universes since the last time you saw them, but if they didn't discreetly let you know when the invitation was issued—"I've cut all cereals right out of my diet, nothing but bean sprouts and almond oil now; you won't believe my skin!"—there's nothing you can do about it. Be prepared to be sorry—but not grief-stricken (after all, you're neither their mother nor a restaurant)—and to suggest they might like some more carrot sticks.

So, to recapitulate, plan to serve nothing that will poison your guests, nothing that will tarnish your reputation, and nothing that you yourself aren't prepared to eat as leftovers for the next week if your guests are more timid than you thought. We suggested above that variety and contrast is as desirable among guests as in what you put on the table. That means that if you're giving them, say, a hot main course of green pasta, you don't want other soft green dishes to accompany it. Lima beans, say, and spinach spoon bread. Crusty bread and an interesting salad sound better.

Work backward to the hors d'oeuvres. Since you're going to be in the kitchen assembling the main course, you probably won't want to serve a first course people have to be at the table for, so it has to be something that's easy to eat and not liable to drip. If the main dish is neither salty nor crisp, bowls of nuts and banana chips might provide that element. If there's a lot of cheese in the sauce, you don't want cheese and crackers as an appetizer. How about some kind of cracker and an eggplant spread. Or smoked oysters. Or a little dish of cherry tomatoes and a smaller saucer of seasoned salt into which they may be dipped? If there's no meat in the main course, slices of some good ham might please people.

Now work forward to the dessert. If your main course was a little heavy on the starches—bread and pasta—a rich cake may not be the best way to go. A lemon sherbet with brownies; or two kinds of cookies and a bowl of fresh fruit might do nicely. When the main course is rich as well as heavy, and unless your guests are all under thirty or have the metabolisms of triatheletes, hold back on the butterfat at dessert. Remember once again: your desire is not to overwhelm your guests with either calories expended—by you—or consumed—by them.

That takes care of the menu. What you will have noticed in reading over ideas about hors d'oeuvres, main course, and dessert is that whether it's simple or not, it all takes time. So keep one of your mental clocks running in the countdown mode, both when you're planning and in the hours before your guests arrive.

When you're issuing the invitations, you'll obviously tell your guests what time you're expecting them to arrive. Come over around 7:00 P.M., you might say, I think we'll be sitting down at 8:00 P.M. This means they can come as early as 7:00 P.M.—if they're both retired, they'll arrive at 7:00 P.M. on the dot—and that if they're the parents of young children and the two-year-old won't go to bed for the sitter, they can show up as late as 8:00 P.M. But the unspoken assumption in American culture is that an invitation to come for dinner doesn't mean guests can show up thirty minutes early because they were in the neighborhood and it was convenient. Nor should they arrive much more than twenty minutes after the appointed hour unless they have a really good reason. Truly virtuous guests will call to explain the delay in advance of their late arrival. Thoughtful hosts or hostesses will know when issuing the invitations who knows how to get to the house and who doesn't. For the latter, she will either find a ride or give directions.

Perhaps one or two of your guests will inquire what sort of dinner it's going to be. Presumably they're not asking what you'll be serving because that's terribly rude. More likely they want to know if it's dressy or casual. Help them out by saying, "Oh, I think we're just going to grill some vegetables in the backyard." Translation: it's casual. Or, "I'm trying a new recipe from *Gourmet's* holiday issue so I thought I might polish the silver and iron some linen." Translation: it might be fun to dress up.

What to do when, at the moment of the invitation, the prospective guest announces that she'll have a cousin visiting or that he already has a date for the evening but perhaps. . . . You have two choices. If you have a pretty clear idea of what kind of party you want to have or your space is limited, politely decline their invitation to bring along someone you haven't had the pleasure of meeting: "What a good idea! I wish I'd gotten that big table I had my eye on. Could I give you a raincheck?" Or if your party for six could just as easily be a party for eight, roll out the red carpet a few more feet.

How about offers to bring something? Again, you have two choices. Say, "Yes" and tell them what. Say, "No" ("That's awfully kind of you but I think I have things pretty well under control") and be prepared for a bottle of wine or a bouquet of flowers. There's a tiny school of thought—tiny and crabby—according to which arriving at a host's door with wine in hand is bad form: the implication is that the host's wine isn't up to the guest's standards so he's brought his own. On the other hand, if you have already raised the Château Margaux from your cellars and brought it to a perfect 68°, you are not required to serve the guest's wine and you are by no means rude to save it for another occasion. Beyond the wine quandary rests the rule, always be prepared to thank your guests for whatever they bring. If you don't care for the wine, the candy, the flowers, somebody will. In this case, it's the thought that counts.

Minutes count more as show time approaches so don't budget your time too precisely. You don't want to be stepping out of the shower if your doorbell rings an unpardonable five minutes early and you don't want to be breathing heavily if everyone arrives at 7:00 P.M. on the dot. Be reasonable: you may know to the minute how long it takes your hair to dry but not how long it takes to sew on an important button that you had been hoping wouldn't fall off. So when you're planning the countdown in your head, allow a little time for the unexpected glitch.

Once your guests do arrive, you'll want to offer them something to drink. You can, if you like, indebt yourself and the next several generations of your family by laying in a stock of spirits and liqueurs and the like such that a guest's most farfetched fancy can be fulfilled. This isn't necessary. You're not a bar.

Offer your guests something to drink and then do the serving yourself. Or, if you're not comfortable mixing drinks, you can set up a bar someplace and invite someone else to help you. Or you can set up a bar—glasses, ice, mixers, and the alcohol itself—and invite people to serve themselves. This way, if guests prefer seltzer to gin, or fruit juice over wine, the gathering will be spared testimonials to AA and those who simply prefer something nonspirituous will be spared knowing looks, or worse, nosy questions.

At the end of the evening, when you've filled the various requests for coffee that's only half decaffeinated or herbal tea made with springwater, you may get offers of help with the dishes. It's your call. How big is your kitchen? How capable are your guests? If it feels like a companionable way to end an informal evening, accept their help. But if you'd rather do the washing up later on or the next day, politely decline the kind offer. Besides, isn't it nicer for them to have spent a pleasant evening during which they haven't had to lift a finger?

When the last cold sip of coffee has been drunk, the final macaroon polished off, and the dregs drained from the last greasy wineglass, your guests will signal that they had no idea what time it was and that they told the sitter they wouldn't be late. Bruce has a fiddle class early the next morning. Wendy's dog has to be driven thirty miles to an obedience class that has yet to do any good. Fine. The good host and hostess accede to their guests' wishes gracefully. Locate the coats. Match them to their owners. See them to the door. Better yet, if you're living in the kind of place where such a gesture is possible, see them to their car or help them get a cab. You musn't, they protest. And if you're a single woman, walking down three flights of stairs to help a rugby-playing guest hail a cab may be ostentatiously above and beyond the call of duty, particularly if he's the first to leave and the rest of the party is left unattended. So be reasonable. But seeing guests to the door, keeping a light on until they're in their car and on their way, shows better manners than closing the door on their heels.

HOW TO WRITE
A THANK-YOU NOTE

❖

Axiom 1: The giver's intention was not to make your life wretched.

Axiom 2: It is logical but incorrect to assume that they gave you whatever they gave you because they wanted to, not in order to be thanked.

Axiom 3: In thank-you notes, as in notes of sympathy or condolence, "Better late than never" is operative. Much time may have elapsed since you received the gift. But the giver will not have forgotten. Would you? You don't need to hear any more about the evils of procrastination. If you're in the habit of putting off until tomorrow what you'd do better to do today, you'll probably keep that habit and your life will be a Moebius strip of guilt and flimsy excuses, panicked haste, and clouded leisure. If, on the other hand, you do what you're supposed to in a reasonable amount of time, you're to be congratulated. One less thing to apologize for.

Etiquette books will tell you to lay in a supply of notecards, 3" × 5". Or that Crane's Moonstone Grey 6" × 8" is the proper size and shade of writing paper. Or that anything but black or dark blue ink is vulgar.

Maybe. Probably. But so what? You have to consider the object of your gratitude. If such details make a big difference to them or if you don't really know the person all that well, the more conservative choice is safer, if not necessarily better. But the point of the thank-you note is not to pass some test, score points on some social checklist, or impress the giver with the depth and richness of your stationery collection. No, the point is to acknowledge that person's kindness to you and that, God forbid, can be done in a pinch on a sheet of ruled paper or on a postcard from Disneyland. Not to do so is rude. Period.

Here are the elements of the acceptable thank-you note: You mention the gift. Or the favor. Or the party. You say you like it or that you had a good time. You express your gratitude. These bare bones, appropriately fleshed out, are within the reach of any seven-year-old. Indeed, a seven-year-old who isn't making some connection between his pleasure and someone else's thoughtfulness is having his education neglected. There is, after all, more to life than finding Delaware on the map.

Here are the elements of the superior thank-you note: Same drill as above but with more feeling. You dilate on the appropriateness of the gift or occasion. ("The new trivet exactly matches a soup tureen of which I'm particularly fond." "The couple I met at dinner had just finished a course I was thinking of taking and the conversation couldn't have been more timely.") You associate this with the person to whom you're writing. ("You always give the best gifts." "You do have a knack for putting interesting people together.") You add the extra paragraph of news or commentary or hope for the future. ("We've all recovered both from our skiing trip and the flu. I don't know which did us in more." "I hope that after the election, Washington will come to its senses.") You conclude the letter.

The ideal, of course, is thanking someone for something you genuinely like. Words will flow onto the well-chosen paper as you imagine they did for Trollope. But that is beside the point. "Like it or not," a phrase that plays through the mind just before "Life's not fair" and on the heels of "We'll see," written thanks are called for regardless of your personal reaction. Remember Ambrose Bierce's cynical definition of politeness: "The most acceptable hypocrisy."